The
Savvy Woman's Guide
to
Owning a Home

Kitty Werner

The Savvy Woman's Guide™ to Owning a Home
by Kitty Werner

Copyright © 2007 Katherine de Marne Werner

One of The Savvy Woman's Guide™ series
Published by:

RSBPress LLC
PO Box 876
Waitsfield VT 05673-0876
www.rsbpress.com

Notice of Rights:

Notice of Liability:

Cover Design: Kitty Werner and Jim Dodds, TreeHouse Group
Book Design: Kitty Werner
Watercolor Painting: "Stone Cottage at Fisk Farm" by Maurie Harrington
Illustrations: Kitty Werner
Photos: Kitty Werner, Peter Werner and Henri de Marne

Printed by Central Plains Book Manufacturers, Winfield, Kansas USA
Printed on New Life Opaque 100% recycled paper

ISBN 10: 0-9710356-1-X
ISBN 13: 978-0-9710356-1-4
Library of Congress Control Number: 2006937761

Printed and bound in the United States of America

0 9 8 7 6 5 4 3 2 1

The Savvy Woman's Mantra

"Nothing is obvious
to the uninformed."

—Salada tea bag tag

Dedication

To my mother, my sister, my daughter,
and women everywhere!

(And to all the males who are brave
enough to admit they haven't a clue.)

Acknowledgments

Books like this don't just "get written," they get done with plenty of help. I couldn't have done this book without the knowledge, experience and wisdom of my husband, Peter, and my father, Henri de Marne, both experts in the construction business.

A special thanks to Sergeant Bob Leary and Chief Bill Jennings of the Berlin Police Department for their help with the emergency, neighborhood and community sections, Bill Elliott of Sugarbush Real Estate, Sharon Kellerman of Graves Real Estate, Karen Blosser and Donna Fuller of State Farm Insurance in Montpelier, as well as anyone else I've missed for their input on their respective chapters.

Thank you to Jake Barickman, fellow thespian and great editor! To Steve Carlson, Upper Access Publishing of Hinesburg VT for his media/publishing savvy.

A big thanks to Kidde, the National Fire Prevention Association and the Red Cross for their advice and help. I hope this makes a difference.

To my writer buddies, Bev, Katherine, Joyce—thanks for always being there.

Thank you, Jim Dodds, for your patience, guidance and help with the design and graphics.

Thank you, Maurie Harrington, your art is an inspiration. To our next project!

Thank you, Pete. One of these days…that car book will get done!

Foreword

How right it is that Kitty should write this book!

Ever since she was a small child, she has demonstrated a great manual dexterity and a keen interest in everything mechanical. As young as seven years old, she helped me build a den and work on other repair jobs around the house even if it meant only handing me tools. A few years later, she helped me enthusiastically and with great excitement in building a special garden shed at our new house. Often she would take things apart to see how they worked and put them back together.

When she and her husband, Peter, built an addition onto their own home, Kitty wired it for electricity, insulated and painted it, as well as helped Peter with the rest of the construction.

Even now, although she has her own house and family, she is always ready to come over and help me with whatever project I need to do.

Over the years she has acquired a considerable knowledge in everything connected to house construction and is finally putting it in a fine book to help women deal with the awesome responsibilities that owning a home can represent.

Henri de Marne

Syndicated columnist, "First Aid for the Ailing House," former builder of fine homes and general remodeling contractor in Potomac MD, author of NAHB book *Entering the Remodeling Field,* contributing editor to Consumer Reports book *Preventive Home Maintenance* and senior consulting editor to Readers Digest *New Do-It-Yourself Manual,* contributing editor to the *Journal of Light Construction,* consultant to homeowners, architects, engineers, builders and condo associations and expert witness on construction litigation cases, home inspector with a combined experience of over 44 years in the building industry. His latest book is taken from over 30 years of his columns, published by Upper Access, *About the House with Henri de Marne.*

A Note about the Second Edition

The original intent of writing this book was to have a homeowner's manual for the uninformed, or new owner. By this time, you should have already purchased your home.

With that in mind, I have removed the chapter on Moving (formerly Chapter 3) and posted it on my website, in case anyone should need it. In its place are two new chapters: Chapter 12—Energy Efficiency and Chapter 13—Going Green. It is my hope that these two chapters will help you, a homeowner, not only save money, but help save our global resources as well.

"Going Green" is a result of my work on the books of an internationally known doctor, Elizabeth Lee Vliet, M.D., who specializes in women's hormones and health issues. Shortly after we met, Dr. Vliet decided she loved the entire Savvy Woman's Guide concept and asked me to produce her books, as Savvy Woman's Guides. She has been a practicing physician for over 20 years treating women for hormone issues, many created by our chemically altered environment. More information about her books and her practice are online at www.herplace.com.

A Note about Resources

Within the text of these pages are references to phone numbers and web-pages. While they are up to date as of this printing, they could change.

The resources will be posted on the RSBPress website and kept as up-to-date as possible.

Visit www.rsbpress.com and click the Resources button.

Contents

Introduction

I'll lay odds that you grew up in a household maintained by someone else, most likely a male, probably Dad. Otherwise, you wouldn't need this book. Don't dwell on it, that's the way we were brought up! Weren't we girls just slated for the kitchen? Cooking in it, not building it. So now you own a home and want to know how it works and what to do if it doesn't work. Congratulations.

To my father's great credit, I, the first of three children—and a female, was the one who helped him build, fix, and maintain our house. Unfortunately, not all children are encouraged, nor interested, in these endeavors.

RELAX, You're not alone

It's okay to feel apprehensive about this ownership thing. You *can* do it. It doesn't take a genius to own and maintain a house. If you (or your partner) aren't handy with a hammer and nail, or comfortable with a power drill, so what! Either learn to do it yourself, befriend someone who is comfortable with wielding the appropriate tool, or learn to find the right professional to do the work for you.

Your maintenance guide

This is where this book enters your life. It was written with you in mind. By homeowners who have been there, done that. Repeatedly. From surviving long, long power outages to replacing bulbs, from overflowing drains to no water at all, we have managed to come through the crises and remain standing (house and all).

PCMT
Years ago, a divorced friend of mine turned to me for help with her old farmhouse. I installed a disposal in her sink, lights in her bathroom and fixed lamps—among other crises. I was Pam's Crisis Management Team.

Give yourself time

As with any new major responsibility, it will take time to "learn the ropes." Every new homeowner has gone through this learning process, and yes, it is perfectly fine to feel overwhelmed at times.

Just as when you purchase a car and have to learn how the lights, wipers, radio, and assorted parts work, the same with a house. The parts are just that much bigger.

Don't be afraid to try

Some jobs are simplicity itself to deal with, others aren't. After reading this, you'll know the difference. There is a huge sense of pride when you know you can do it yourself, and it works. Don't ever underestimate yourself, or your intelligence. Don't let anyone else do that either.

Pick the important stuff

Some of the topics won't concern you, depending on your heating system (most are covered in this book and most houses only have one), or water supply (town supplied or your own well) and other variations. Pick out the sections that concern you and your house, maybe highlight the ends of the pages for quick reference, and learn those.

You do have time for this. The house, barring major catastrophes, will be there for a while, long enough for you to sort this all out. Relax and enjoy the read.

Welcome to the world of homeownership!

P.S. We are assuming that you are an intelligent person, single or otherwise, who needs this knowledge to maintain a home. Marital status has nothing to do with this, as there are men who can't change a light bulb or identify a hammer. Knowledge is power, use it.

Never Too Late

When my mother turned 65, I gave her a little tool kit—her first and only. It is a lightweight, inexpensive collection of simple tools. My poor father went nuts! Mom was now hanging pictures and fixing the odd, pesky door hinge. She was empowered! It was a revelation to her.

Part I

Before You Move

Chapter 1

First Things First

Yes, you have looked at the house, studied it, had it professionally inspected, and hopefully been over it with that fine-toothed comb before you purchased your prize.

But, have you been around the neighborhood? Do you know where your house is in relation to the shopping, the post office, schools, and recreation facilities?

Have you turned on everything that is supposed to be turned on? Aside from your excitement and trepidation.

We'll show you how to start your new life, from getting the real address for your new home, to turning on the power. Moving into a new home is time consuming; getting the furniture organized; if you have children, getting registered in schools; and finding the right fit for everyone. It isn't always easy, but we'll point you in the right directions. It will take work on your part, but that can be the most fun of all—new friends and new activities.

An important note: When we talk about "towns" we are using the term liberally by referring to your community, whether it be a city, a suburb, or out in the countryside. Cities are made up of individual communities and many communities prefer to keep their own identity.

Cool Tip
Get a copy of a local phone book. Not only does it have the usual Yellow Pages, but many have plenty of information about your new community to get you started.

First Things First

Notifying Everyone

You may know where you are going, but does anyone else know how to find you? To be on the safe side, do a bit of homework.

Do It List

Sounds Stupid but–
Check your address! One couple, given their address from their landlord, found out from the electric company that their service was to a slightly different address—in fact, their actual mailing address!

- *Make accurate directions to your house.* If you have to physically get in your car and drive the route, with someone writing down everything as you go, do it.

- *Make sure your house number is easily seen from the street*—in easy-to-read-at-night reflective numbers. If it isn't, make a small sign and post it somewhere visible to emergency services.

- *Stop by the post office* and introduce yourself, double check that your address is correct and above all, get a Change of Address kit and use it. Getting the entire correct 9-digit zip-coded address will make life easier for your mail and you in the long run.

- *Write or visit your Department of Motor Vehicles.* You only have 30 days to make the changes. If you write, include: name, date of birth, license number, and old and new addresses of *each* driver.

- *Notify your insurance company.* If you are moving from a city, you may find your rates have gone down. Some insurance companies will notify everyone you ask them to. They will then change your car registrations and drivers licenses.

- *Use your personal mailing list* to notify your friends in advance of your move, that way your personal mail will arrive at the right place.

- *Don't forget your magazines and newspapers.* Magazines and newspapers take up to six weeks before your new address change takes effect. And not all periodicals will be forwarded.

How do you get your mail?

The mail carrier is responsible for the safe delivery of your mail. If he or she can't guarantee your box will safely hold your mail, he or she won't deliver it. After all, who will be the first to complain if the mail is soaked, mutilated, or lost? You. If the box is rusted or decrepit, not in the correct spot (say a snowplow or car hit it), or the snow is piled in front of the box, the carrier is not obliged to deliver the mail to that box until the situation is corrected.

City and suburbs

This one is obvious. Suburban or city folk have a carrier on foot who drops mail in a box attached to the house, or a slot in the door.

The size of the box or slot is fairly standard. Older houses should already have a mail slot or box installed at the correct height. If you don't have one already, ask the carrier where to install your box, or if he or she has a preference. That is their decision.

If you wish to install a slot, don't make it too big as it can invite unwanted intrusions. Boxes and slots are available at hardware and building-supply stores.

Post office boxes

If you prefer to have a post office box number, of course, now is the time to apply for it. There could be a waiting list, so have a Plan B. PO boxes are located within the front of the post office itself. In many post offices the front section is open longer hours than the main office. Make note of the hours if they are different.

Rural deliveries

In the "sticks," it's a rural carrier putting mail in boxes in a designated location, or you pick it up yourself at the post office.

Main Point
A carrier is not required to deliver to a box that isn't secure or safe for your mail. That means: dry, accessible, in a closed "safe" container.

Are you a creative type and don't yet have a box? Make your own. Within bounds, of course. It still has to follow the rules and be acceptable by your carrier.

If you need a rural box, the carrier will tell you where to put it up. They are only required to deliver along town roads, not private ones, i.e., driveways. You are required to install the box at a specific height so the carrier can reach it from his or her vehicle without getting out. That is written in their contract; that is the law. The minimum height is around 50 inches, the maximum is around 54 inches. The final say rests with your carrier.

Boxes come in several "U.S. Post Office approved" sizes with the small one the most commonly used. They, too, can be purchased at hardware and building-supply stores. If you get many catalogs or packages, for your sake and that of your carrier, use a larger size box.

Do It List

Put your address on your box in clear, easy-to-read numbers and letters you can purchase from the hardware store. Carriers do take vacations and substitute carriers won't know the route as well as the regular carrier. If you only want your box number on the outside of your box, put your name and number inside the box for the benefit of a non-regular carrier.

Calling for Help

While it may not sound important in the rush of activities, you still need to know where the emergency and health services are for your area: that is, ambulance/rescue, hospitals, fire department, doctors, dentists, veterinarians, etc. You need to know how to contact them, they need to know how to find you. If E911 is working in your area the "how to get to you" should be taken care of. But do you know how to find the fastest way to the hospital? Or how to find the vet if your pet is injured?

To help your children:

If you live in a smaller community, take your children to visit the local police station or fire house. It will help them understand where these services are and who will be coming to help when they're needed.

If your children are too young to read, sign up for speed-calling or program your telephone with numbers corresponding to pictures of appropriate objects or people (i.e., Mom at the office, fire truck) and post it near the phone, written big enough for the smallest child to use. Even a four-year-old can handle pictures and number buttons.

Police

Not all areas are covered by the same law enforcement services. The state police generally cover everywhere in a state, although in a few states they may only handle state highway enforcement. Law enforcement is handled on the state level, the county level (usually the sheriff's department), then on more local levels. Most cities have their own police force, even some towns have their own, depending on the size of the town. Some small towns may subcontract services from the county sheriff's department.

Save Your Own Life
Program the speed dial using the outside numbers on the keypad (1, 3, 7 and 9) for the most urgent numbers as they are the easiest to pick out.

E911
If Enhanced 911 is used in your area, use it for emergencies only. For areas not served by E911, the local phone book will have the numbers to use.

Go for a visit

It stands to reason that smaller communities have smaller police departments. Usually, they are much more open to visits from new families. A precinct in New York City probably wouldn't be excited about more people milling around their space, but smaller community law enforcement departments tend to welcome visits. Call and ask. The officers will then know the children if called to help and the children will feel comfortable with their new pals, the friendly officers.

When you visit your local police department, see what's on the public bulletin board. Do they post the names and addresses of people on vacation or other confidential information? Or is that information kept confidential? Not everyone visiting the police station is a "good" guy. If you think this isn't so, this came from a police chief.

Ask about places that you shouldn't walk or drive through at night. Are there any danger spots to avoid? Are there certain sections of town or your community that should be avoided at night? During the day? Is that community path a safe place at night? It is better to be forewarned.

Fire Department

The fire department usually handles *just* fires: chimney fires, house fires, brush fires; if it's burning, call the fire department. If it isn't an emergency, don't call the emergency number. Use the non-emergency number in the phone book. No, don't call fire companies to rescue cats stuck in trees—call Animal Rescue.

Prevention Services for Children

Most fire companies prefer to do their prevention training directly with children via school programs. If your school system hosts a program, see what ages it covers. Usually these programs are aimed at early elementary grades hoping the children will take the information back home. You can always call the station directly

Heads Up
Each state's law enforcement set up is different. You need to find out about your area's situation, and the best way to do that is to visit the department.

Important
Everyone living in your house must know about fire safety. Even kids can learn the basics and save their own lives. Visit Kidde's website (see Resources) for games designed to teach children fire safety.

(non-emergency number only) and ask about programs or a possible visit. Perhaps your children missed the school program for the year, and, wisely, you'd rather not wait for the next program to start. See Chapter 15—Get Out Alive for more information on preparing for fire emergencies.

Ambulance

Is your ambulance a private company? Or is it a municipal? Some areas have several competing ambulance services; others have volunteer providers, particularly in rural areas. Again, if you are in a E911 area, then the choices are handled by E911.

Another note about where the services come from: in many locales, if you live on or near a town line, you may call the service just blocks away from you, only to find out that the services sent came from miles away. That's because of contracts, coverage areas, and other issues. Of course, it would take longer for the distant service to show up, costing valuable minutes. Find out exactly who will be answering your calls, as well as how long it might take to get to you.

Consider signing up for training classes. Many offer evening classes in CPR, emergency rescue training, beginning and advanced first aid, and other courses that could prepare you for an EMT certificate.

If your community ambulance is a volunteer effort, join it, by paying dues, as a supporting member. Many companies will give you a free ride if you ever need it. Your donation is much less than paying the cost of a ride in an emergency later. And it may be tax deductible.

Hospitals

You need to know not only which hospital is closest to you, but does it have a trauma unit? Are they prepared to handle children specifically in their trauma unit? This can be critical if your child is involved in a serious accident. What about your doctor or primary care

Good to Know Find out just where that ambulance is coming from... the closer, the better

Volunteer Make yourself available if there is ever a need for your services, say for a search and/or rescue. The more hands to call on, the more ground can be covered quickly.

providers? Are they affiliated with this hospital? If not, with which hospital are they affiliated?

If anyone in the family has a chronic illness, which hospital or health care provider best handles the illness? Where is the hospital or office and what is the fastest way to get there?

When your children are enrolled in school, you may be asked: To which hospital would you like your children taken in an emergency? While it may seem obvious to you, your choice of hospital may not be the choice of the ambulance crew at the time of an accident. As a parent, perhaps you want the victim transported directly to a specific hospital. Make sure the ambulance personnel know that. Make sure the school or activity your child participates in knows what you want them to do.

Poison Control Center

Especially if you have small children and pets, this number can be a lifesaver. Your local Poison Control Center number is in your phone directory. Add it to your speed-dialing collection.

Call your local number as a first defense when someone (or pet, as 25% of their calls are for pets) swallows or chews something inappropriate. One example: Our then two-year-old daughter ate a small flashlight bulb. Horrified, we called the Poison Control Center. We were told that she would survive with no action on our part as the bulb was essentially harmless. She did. But who else would you have called?

In larger cities the listings for the Poison Control Center include a non-emergency education number. Call it for information about dealing with poisons. Log onto the main website at www.aapcc.org for even more information about poison control centers, including the one nearest you.

Game Wardens, ASPCA, Humane Society, and Animal Rescue

Your community should have at least one of the above services. These are the people to call if you find a cat up a tree or your pet is lost. These services care for wild, abandoned, or injured animals (or find someone who will) if you should find an orphaned creature.

Humane Societies offer pets for adoption for a reasonable fee that covers a health check-up, shots, spaying or neutering. If you want a pet, here is the place to go first.

Game Wardens are a more rural law enforcement job. Wardens handle larger animals that stray into the wrong places, monitor hunting activities, and rescue and care for orphaned creatures.

Just in Case
Call any of these animal rescue organizations if you witness any animal cruelty. *This is a crime.*

Doctors, Dentists, Vets

When you move, your insurers or HMO may dictate which health-care providers you can use. They will offer you a list of providers in your new area, but it is up to you to do the visiting and decide to which providers you will entrust your family. This choice is not to be taken lightly.

Ask for referrals from your current providers. The medical network is extensive. Ask your co-workers or friends if they have any suggestions.

Check out the credentials of each provider. With Internet access, this is particularly easy. Log onto the American Board of Medical Specialties at www.abms.org or call them at 1-866-ASK-ABMS. Another site to check out, AMA Physician Select at www.ama-assn.org offering basic directory information.

Choose doctors who are Board Certified. That means they have taken years of extra training in specific specialties. Matching doctor's specialties to your family's interests provides you with better health care. If there are athletes in the family, it helps if your doctor is one too.

Heads UP
The same advice goes for dentists and vets. Everyone should be comfortable with the new providers, pets included. If you don't trust the provider, how do you expect your family or pet to trust them?

Make appointments to visit each office. If you, or one of your family members, don't feel comfortable with the practicing physicians, go to the next office. You are choosing the doctors who will be handling your health issues and those of your family. They are the ones who will be coordinating your annual physicals, immunization programs for your children and managing any health problems with other providers in the future.

Free or Fair?

If the office charges you an office visit, that's fair, too. You wouldn't offer your services for free either.

Questions for the office visit:

- *Are the office hours convenient for you?*

- *Do they hold evening office hours?*

- *Who takes the off-hour emergency calls?* Is it someone you like or trust? What if it isn't? Can you call someone else? Can you go directly to the emergency room?

- *How close and convenient are they for you to reach?*

- *Do their specialties match your requirements and needs?*

- *Are you comfortable speaking with the provider or do you tend to hold back?* Does the doctor speak to you as an intelligent person and discuss any issues with you? Or does he or she talk down to you or expect you to let them handle it?

- *What hospital are they affiliated with?* Do they routinely use that hospital? (See about Hospitals in the previous section.) Are you comfortable with that choice?

Chapter 2

Get Functional

It's a certainty that the previous owners of the house will have turned off or arranged the end of their responsibility for the utilities connected to your new home. Therefore, it is up to you to call these companies and open your own account at your home. If you had a previous account with this utility company ask them to transfer your account, so you shouldn't need to pay another deposit.

Find out when the meter reader comes around. If the reader regularly comes at the end of the month and a stranger shows up at a different time asking to be let in, call the company first, before allowing the suspicious "reader" anywhere. Verify the person's identity and any credentials with the company directly. Ask the company what the credentials should be, or look like, and ask if this person is one of their employees.

Our electric company just switched to scannable meters, that can be read from the driveway. If your company has upgraded, yet someone is coming to "read a meter" inside your home—be very wary!

In an apartment or rental situation, you probably only had to pay electric as well as telephone bills. Now it will be up to you to manage the heating, cooling (if any), snowplowing and sanding (in the northern climes), water, power, and anything else that makes the house function.

Get Turned On!

Home-work
Do your math homework before signing up for special electric rates. Or have the electric company run some figures for you to make sure you really will save money. In the end, we didn't save anything and switched back. To really save on utility bills, check with your suppliers or the state about their energy efficiency programs.

Take notes as you do this—write down the names of the people you contacted and when, for each company. It doesn't hurt to get to know them, at least a little, especially if it is a small company.

Electric

Call the local company and get signed up and the power turned on. If you are in a state with choices, check all the companies out before choosing.

You should have this done so the power is on before you move in. You want to make sure that all the appliances and fixtures work correctly before you load them up. Nothing like loading up a dishwasher, turning it on and having it spew water all over your kitchen floor.

Ask the electric company if they have special rates for setback times, ripple or on-peak/off-peak rates. If you are willing to do your most electricity-consuming chores during off hours, you may save a bundle.

Do It List

Do a check of all the light fixtures. Are they all there and working? Or did the previous owner take the fixtures and you need to replace them. Do the replacing before you move in.

Buy plenty of bulbs, more than you think you could possibly need. Fill all the empty sockets and test the sockets and switches.

Piped in fuel and water

If you are connected to a municipal water supply, call the water company and sign up for an account. If you have a private well, don't worry about this call.

Similarly, you probably don't have a choice when it comes to piped in fuel. Call the appropriate company and open your account.

Fuel in tanks

If you see big tanks around the house, they hold fuel for something important *in* your house. Many water heaters, heating systems, cook stoves and other appliances are run by propane or natural gas, or oil. If it isn't piped in, the fuel is housed in blah-looking tanks either next to the house, in the basement, underground or stashed discreetly out of view—but still accessible to the supplier's truck.

Find out who owns the tank the fuel is stored in. It isn't uncommon, at least in rural states, for the fuel company to loan you the tank used at your house. If you change companies, the tank is removed by the former supplier.

If you find you need a bigger tank, that is easy enough to arrange—if the tank is on loan. Otherwise, you need to buy a larger tank.

If you own the tank, check it occasionally to make sure it isn't leaking.

Find out if your water heater is leased or rented from your supplier. Ditto with some propane heaters. For example, our own water and propane heaters are leased monthly from one supplier. When we decided to change companies, instead of having the first company remove the equipment, we bought out our leases. It cost less in time and hassle. Although, it may pay to haggle rental equipment rates if you change companies, or buy your own equipment and have it installed. For more information on replacing any of this equipment, see Chapter 9.

Don't be afraid to ask around and call different suppliers. Compare reputations as well as prices. While one supplier may have a great "special" when you call, do ask how long it lasts. Don't be afraid to bargain and use one supplier against another. (Same for buying a car.)

Leaks! Watch for leaks if you have fuel tanks. If you find a leak, the tank will have to be replaced. Plus the clean-up could be expensive!

Try these for questions:

- Are you under a contract? If so, for how long?
- Must you sign another contract?

What happens when the contract expires? Does the price soar or fluctuate with the market?

What happens if you are under contract for one rate and the rates drop?

Cold Weather Notice

In cold climes, do not let the tank empty to less than 20% full—will make it difficult for the pressure in the tank to force the liquid into the lines to the appliance.

Don't count on those extra gallons as a buffer. They may not get to their appointed appliance when you need it.

If deliveries are only a few times a year (if you have a large tank instead of a smaller one) does it cost you more or less per gallon? Usually costs more. I argued about this with one of our suppliers as we were buying the same amount of propane over one year, just having it delivered twice a year up our nasty dirt road versus monthly deliveries up our nasty dirt road. We reckoned it would be easier to handle the road twice in good weather, instead of all year round including during blizzards. I did talk them down 40 cents a gallon once, before we switched to a more reasonable supplier.

How much fuel do you need to buy before you hit the next tier of "cheaper" rates? If you are only using a few gallons to cook with versus using over 500 gallons a year for heating, cooking, and other appliances, perhaps you should reconsider either the fuel used or switch appliances. If you prefer cooking with gas, but are being charged too much for the fuel, consider either adding another appliance (say, heater or water heater) or changing to an electric stove. Quantities under 500 gallons a year have been charged far more than over that amount.

Will you get a discount for paying within two days or so? We have the bill automatically charged to our credit card and get an additional 5 cents off per gallon.

What happens if the tank goes "dry" in the off, non-business, hours? How much does that cost in extra charges? It is usually considered an emergency delivery and therefore warrants more money in labor and charges.

Does the supplier deliver regularly? Or will they deliver on a "will-call as needed" basis. It is better to have it delivered regularly. Then there are no surprises. In cold climes, we are warned that letting the tank empty to less than 20% full will make it difficult for the pressure in the tank to force the liquid into the lines to the appliance. So, don't count on those extra gallons as a buffer. They may not get to their appointed appliance when you need it.

ɜ❧ If you sign a contract, does it cover replacement, repair, and outage problems? It had better, as the equipment is theirs, not yours to repair and maintain. When our water heater died one weekend, we didn't have to pay the repair charges; it was in our contract for them to maintain their equipment, in a timely fashion—at their expense. Those weekend repairs cost the earth, so this is a plus.

ɜ❧ Will the supplier come and inspect the equipment on a yearly basis? Depending on the equipment, this is a huge bonus. Some equipment doesn't require much care and feeding aside from vacuuming regularly during the season it is used. Other equipment must be inspected and maintained regularly by experts.

Periodically check the capacity gauge of your fuel tank yourself and keep an eye on the level. Markings are in a percentage of the capacity of the tank. If the level seems level, or rather too level, tap the gauge. I wouldn't go so far as to tell you to whack the thing, but if the gauge doesn't move, call the supplier and tell them.

Humor Lines

If you are into decorating the tanks, ask the supplier first. Ours told us we could paint it whatever we wanted, except for writing the word "bomb" on it. They drew their sense-of-humor line at that one.

We once diligently watched our propane tank's gauge throughout the summer and were thrilled that with only the water heater using propane we weren't really "using any"! The level stayed level. Until the October cold snap and the propane heater didn't work. Adding insult to the injury, it was considered an emergency delivery—for an extra charge. We talked them out of the extra charge as their equipment was faulty. Then we changed companies.

Get Safe

One of the first jobs to do in your new home is to install, if not already in place: smoke detectors, fire extinguishers and carbon monoxide detectors.

The second thing to do is make all those repairs the inspection report told you were most necessary. If you don't do them before you move in, they probably won't get done.

Clean the chimney flues, and make sure the furnace or heating system is in working order.

Repair the reparable

If your home inspection report showed any problems with the house, now is the time to make the repairs. Not after you move in, unless it is a relatively minor repair that can be put off. Ask the inspector for his or her opinion. Minor repairs are one thing, major ones must be tackled immediately.

If the chimney needs repair, fix it immediately. Broken, cracking or spalling masonry is a danger. If the chimney flashing is leaking that can cause your roof to fail as well. Don't take a chance on ruining your furniture and other treasures.

If the roof needs repair, get it done now.

Clean those chimney pipes

This job can't be stressed enough. Even if the job was done at the end of the last season, or the previous owner swears it was just done, at least have it checked again for your peace of mind. If the house was sitting around waiting to be sold, an animal could have made a home in your chimney. Or maybe third-degree (aka Class III, the heavy baked-on or hard-glazed) creosote lines the flue.

You don't know that until you find a certified chimney sweep to inspect it for you.

Save Your Own Life

Fixing any roof problems now can save you a fortune later.

Fixing a chimney *now* could save your life.

Results of not following proper codes

Charred wood—it takes about 10 years of use before wood actually burns.

The flue crumbled allowing the gases to escape into the lower chimney mass and start burning the wood forms (the burned ceiling) left inside. Those forms should have been removed—for safety.

This photo shows what can be lurking behind that nice block wall in your basement. There was a thimble in the wall where the lower arrow points to the flue. The thimble was not the required 18" away from combustibles, nor was there a heat shield to protect the floor above the pipes from the furnace going through the thimble into the flue beyond. There is a fuel pipe hidden in there. Imagine if that had blown.

Arrange to have an inspection, if not another sweeping done, and then make an appointment for the next sweeping.

Finding a good sweep can be a lifesaver. Check the Yellow Pages, or ask friends with chimneys and woodstoves, who they would recommend. Also check with stores that sell fireplace equipment and supplies or woodstoves for a recommended sweep.

A sweep may not be equipped, nor experienced, in chimney repairs, but they should be able to tell you when a chimney isn't working correctly or needs repairs. Some sweeps do have the training for minor repairs. At the very least, the sweep can recommend a mason qualified to do any repairs.

Another note about masons: some are better than others. In most locations, you don't need any formal training to be a mason. Just a trowel, something to mix in, and nerve.

Careful

A young couple bought an old farmhouse during the summer months, fixed it up and moved in. Come September and the first cold spell, they lit their "new" wood-stove and burned their house out. No one was hurt, but they never returned. They hadn't checked and/or cleaned the chimney.

Okay, so I harp on keeping any chimneys clean. As Peter is a mason, and builds, as well as repairs them, we know only too well what happens when a chimney fire gets out of hand, and/or burns a house down.

Therefore, only choose a reputable mason whose work you have seen or whose work has been standing for many years and is still in excellent condition. Choose a mason who has had adequate training, is used, well-liked, as well as respected, by general contractors whose living and reputation is founded on his subcontractors as well as his own employees. Do your research well. Anyone can build a chimney, but not just anyone can build a safe one.

Check with your insurance agent to see if he or she has any recommendations. While agents aren't, by law, allowed to recommend just one mason or contractor, they can steer you in the right direction if there are many choices.

Hang on to that paperwork

You do need to collect and store all your paperwork (insurance papers, mortgage deeds, loan records, titles, etc.) in a safe, accessible location.

Can you get a copy of the house plans? Excellent. If you ever need to track down just where the electric lines run, or plumbing pipes go, where else but in the house plans? More on that in Part II—Get to Know Your House.

Ever want to build an addition? Adding new lights? Remodeling? Grab those house plans, if you have them. They are the structural and historical records of your house.

Do It List

- *Call* on the electric, telephone, any fuel companies necessary to get your house functional.

- *Copy* down the names, addresses, phone numbers, account numbers associated with your house.

- *Install or check existing smoke and fire detectors, and extinguishers.* If you don't have them, get them and install them immediately!

- If you have a chimney, get it checked or swept now!

- *Repair any roof problems*—before they get too big to handle.

Chapter 3

Visit Your Town Offices

The hub of any community is the Town or City Hall. That is where the selectboard, planning commission, and zoning board meetings are held; and where tax collecting, registering, and permitting are done. The mayor and/or town manager's offices are here as well. In short, any questions you have or anything else to do with your new community will be handled here.

Where to pay those taxes

Local property taxes, the bane of homeowners, are paid to the town. If the state has its own property taxes, you pay them directly to the state. You will be billed for these taxes, don't worry. They won't forget you. And if you don't pay on time, ouch! The interest charges and fines pile up rapidly.

To ease your pain about paying those taxes, they are used for your benefit. They pay for schools, libraries, road repairs, plowing and sanding, recreation facilities, beautification, or whatever *you vote to do* with the funds.

When you first visit the town office, check to be sure the taxes are current on your new property. Verify that, indeed, the former owners had paid up to the time they sold the house. If not, you may be liable for any unpaid taxes and/or fines due.

Try This
While at the office, pick up the latest Town or City Report. It will give you a complete picture of your community including telling you where the tax dollars are spent and why. And also if there are any plans for major changes coming your way.

Property taxes are usually paid on a schedule; all at once, or perhaps several payments. Trust me, they will bill you. Plan your savings for this big chunk of money well ahead of time so you aren't caught short. If your mortgage doesn't include paying the taxes (that is, the bank is collecting the taxes in escrow), it is entirely up to you to deliver the goods on time. Get a receipt for each payment.

If there is a rebate program on property taxes, you need a receipt for the allowable part of your property. In Vermont, for example, the allowable portion of property taxes currently cover a "homestead and up to two acres" only. If you live in a planned suburb of less acreage per house than that, your whole tax bill is covered. Your tax bill should reflect how much of the property is considered homestead. You may need a receipt to send in with your tax return for this too.

Register to vote!

With the Motor-Voter Laws now in place, you can register to vote at the Department of Motor Vehicles, but registering at your town office has a decidedly more "formal" feel to it. Anyway you do it, register!

While any and all voices are important in a community, the smaller the town, the more essential your voice. If this doesn't make sense to you, consider this: years ago, I was asked to fill a vacancy as one of the three town auditors for a year. Come election time, I hadn't planned to run for auditor, much less anything else. As it required only six votes to elect someone to an office (if unopposed), I was "re-elected" several years in a row by helpful, proud family members! My name wasn't even on the ballot.

Take part in town meetings

They are an education in your town's future as well as its past. Don't try to change anything immediately. First, learn about your town, about its zoning process, about its own plans for the future. If you have big plans for the town, get in sync with the rest of the community before launching any projects.

Home Office?

If you have a home office that can legitimately be deducted on your Federal income tax Form 8829, get a tax receipt. You won't need it to file with your return, but you should have a copy for your records.

Speak up

Likewise, if you see something about to happen to your town that you don't like, *say something!* And the place to do it is at the town offices. That's what Zoning Board and Planning Commission meetings are about. They are usually open to the public with meetings held on a regular schedule. Agendas for these meetings are posted at the offices. By law, the town must post warnings of special hearings in the local paper. If you have a gripe, take it to the proper meeting or hearing.

Parking and plowing regulations

If you have moved into a "land of snow" there are bound to be regulations on where you can park during when the snow falls. Northern cities and towns have regulations posted on telephone poles and lampposts telling you when and where you can't park during snow storms. Some cities have flashing lights. Plowers can't plow if the streets are covered with parked cars. If you park on the street during a snowstorm in a marked area, you will be towed, at your expense. If there are bans in your area, make plans ahead of time for the safe parking of your vehicles.

Register "Rover"

All dogs, and in some areas, cats and other domesticated pets, must be registered with the town. If a dog strays from home, the tag number will tell the right people where to find you to return your pet. You will need an up-to-date rabies certificate from your vet along with a copy to be filed with the town. Be sure to put the rabies tag on your pet's collar along with the town's tag. There is usually a small fee to have a pet registered. If a pet is spayed or neutered, the fee is less. If you don't pay by the deadline, the fees go up dramatically. Register on time.

Registering your dog not only helps you and your pet, but if your pet ever bites someone, then the authorities know that your pet is rabies free and won't have to be killed to verify that.

Don't Let Them Get Away With It! There are countless stories of people moving into a new community who "know better" what the community really needs.

Don't be one of them.

Leash laws—live with them

Find out about local leash laws. Even in the country with endless acres of forest and fields to play in, there are likely to be leash laws. Quite simply, is your dog allowed out alone to roam? Probably not. Can you stop your dog from chasing something if it isn't on a leash? Dogs should be under the control of a person at all times.

Must your pet be contained on your own property? Do you use a fence, or a running chain?

In areas with deer population, leash laws are particularly important to protect the deer herds in winter. Loose dogs gather in frenzied packs to chase deer. As the snow gets deeper and develops a crust, the lighter-weight dogs have the decided advantage over the heavier deer with pointed hooves. Dogs will chase deer to utter exhaustion and collapse. What's left of the deer carcass isn't pretty. Don't think your dog is above all this. You'd be amazed at which dogs run deer. Even the sweetest and most innocent looking do it. Be forewarned that the game warden has the right to shoot any dog caught in the act. Even if it is yours.

Taking out the trash

Think you can just chuck your bagged trash out on your front lawn and someone will happily remove it for you? Not always and not everywhere! If there is trash and recycling pickup, ask these questions:

- What days of the week and at what time is the pickup expected?
- How do the sanitation engineers want it left out and where?
- What sort of bags or containers should you use?
- If there are specific bags or containers, where do you get them?
- If recycling is included, do you bag it?
- Or do you put it in special containers?
- And where do you get these containers?

Smart Trick?

If you own a dog and would like it to have some freedom, consider the "radio" fences now available. Some cost under $100 and do work with most dogs. Be aware that thick fur around the animal's neck may render the collar device useless.

If you don't have a community-wide and paid-for waste collection system then it is up to you to deal with the mess. Ask your town clerk or manager about the options. Perhaps there are trash companies that will come and collect your trash for a monthly fee. You must call them and ask to join their route. They, too, will have requirements for what can be picked up and what can't. Ask the same questions as above. You might wish to check around if there are several companies. They don't all charge the same price. Ask if there are other options. If you don't produce a lot of trash on a monthly basis, have them pick up only once or twice a month instead of weekly. If you are big trash producers (say you have a home office or other business), then maybe you need your own container.

If you have a less-than-weekly pickup, will the company pick up your trash from a storage container on your property? Having several weeks of garbage stored in your house can get revolting. Storage sheds are a great alternative and many companies are happy to remove the properly bagged trash from your own shed.

If you live in a rural area, much of this trash disposal business is left up to you to deal with. There will be an authorized landfill you can use. Or perhaps a local trash and recycling center. We take our recycling to our local recycling center and pay so much per bag of garbage, and unload the recyclables for free. In many places, you don't even have to sort the recyclables anymore. Just bundle them up together and chuck them in the appropriate container.

Recycling other than throwing out

If you have access to the internet, join Freecycle. As a member, you either Offer items you want to clear out of your house, or ask for something you need, as Wanted. Those who answer make the arrangements with you to deliver, or pick up the items. Nothing is ever sold, nor is money requested. (www.freecycle.org)

Recycled
This book is printed on New Life recycled paper. No new trees were cut down, just your waste white paper was used.

Recycling Center
Set up a recycling area in your own house and teach everyone how to clean and store the stuff until ready for pickup or delivery. That way you aren't stuck with mounds of recycling to deal with at the last minute.

What can you recycle?
Each waste facility has a list of what recyclables they will take. It's worth keeping it handy to refer to when something unusual is headed for the trash.

We've unloaded metal to a sculptor (he thought he was picking up a kitchen mixer, but got a cement mixer instead—he was in scrap-metal heaven), an exercise bike, old TVs, bags of outgrown clothing, plastic shelving, and excess kitchen items. Not to mention helping a new family stock their kitchen with a microwave, dishes, and assorted items, but also passed on a complete computer system.

Kitchen scraps

If you don't have a compost pile yet, make one! You can clean out just about all your food wastes and create some seriously good garden soil with it. We've been doing this for years. Not only do we get great soil, but we have lightened our waste load considerably. You don't need to buy anything to make one. Find a sunny corner in your yard somewhere and dump the kitchen scraps in a pile. Cover the pile with enough dirt to hide the new wastes. In warm weather, it takes a couple of weeks to create some usable soil.

The Savvy Woman's Guide™ to Gardening will have more on gardening and composting for beginning gardeners.

Naughty, naughty
It is against the law to burn trash outside. Even paper trash.

Consider your own health and that of your family.

The inks, especially in colored papers, are poison. And you will be breathing it.

What to do with hazardous waste?

Old paint, turpentine, car oil, batteries, poisons, the list grows daily. Don't just heave these into the trash, unless your town pickup regulations say you can. Many communities, in conjunction with the local landfill, will host a Hazardous Waste Day where you can bring in all that stored crud from your garage or basement to a designated location and unload it safely. Watch for announcements in your local paper, or call the town hall for information.

DO NOT pour any of this stuff down a drain! If you are hooked up to a municipal water system, that poison is heading straight into your water supply. If you use a septic system, you could destroy it incurring great expense to repair the damage. Those poisons will haunt you in the future. They are, in fact, killing us slowly.

Permits—What you need for what

Gone are the days when you can just burn leaves, sell off your unused stuff, build things without asking or telling or getting permission to do so. It's the law, folks. Permits are required so that the community can keep an eye on what's going on.

Lawn sales

Holding a once-in-a-while yard-garage-tag-lawn sale is one thing, but supposing, and this has happened, that the sale "happens" in one spot every week. That "sale" is now considered a business and needs to be taxed as such. Therefore, if you wish to hold a one-time sale, check with the town hall to see if you need a permit to do so. If you hold too many of these sales, then you are in business and need to collect sales tax, report it, and send it in. Ask the town offices about the necessity of permits for any random sale.

Burning leaves, burning anything

I remember living in the suburbs and come fall, my mother and the three of us kids would rake all the leaves into a pile, jump on the mound, scatter and re-rake it until it was time to burn it all. We even had our pictures taken for the *Washington Post* while we stood proudly around our pile of fallen, brittle autumn booty. Nowadays, you need to ask about permits. The words "forest fire" strike fear into anyone with property to lose. The danger is real. Burning cinders lazily floating upwards can land anywhere—and burn it. "It" could even be your own beautiful shake roof.

Fires can and do get out of hand too quickly for a single person to deal with. You must be prepared for this with a hose ready to pour on the fire, and what ever else is recommended by your Fire Warden. If the ground is dry, don't even think of burning anything, anywhere. Take it to the dump.

Do not, under any circumstance, attempt to burn any construction debris, plastics, carpeting or other leftovers without getting permission—even if you are allowed to.

Watch Out! Hazardous Waste is called Hazardous Waste because it can kill you. Don't even think of pouring anything hazardous into the ground or burying it. If you spill it, clean it up, thoroughly. If it is truly bad, contact the authorities immediately.

Nature's compost Think about it, trees drop their leaves to fertilize themselves for next year.

This is all dump material. And possibly special dump material. You must ask if you can dump the stuff at your local landfill. If you burn any of this, you are poisoning the air around you including your family, the neighbors, and your community.

Depending on where you live, needing a permit may not be an issue. The only way to find out is to ask at the Town/City Hall or Offices. If you have a Forest Fire Warden, you likely need a permit to burn anything outside.

Remember

Whatever is in that smoke, will get into your lungs.

House additions

If you add on to your house, you need a permit. That is so the Town Listers can come and re-assess your house for tax purposes. Listers are the people who put a price on the value of your home for the Grand List—the tax rolls. Always check in with the Town Office before adding or changing anything permanent to your home. There will be more on this subject in Chapter 22—Planning is Everything.

Find out what the laws are regarding what is considered a taxable structure. Does the structure need a foundation to qualify as taxable? For example, in our town, if a structure doesn't have a foundation, it isn't taxed as part of the homestead's value (homestead meaning the home itself and surrounding acreage). Therefore, a small shed simply sitting on the ground isn't taxable. But a big, proper garage with a foundation certainly would be. Consider this when making any plans for outside storage.

Do-It List

- ꙮ Register to vote, and register your pets
- ꙮ Know what permits are needed for what
- ꙮ Find out how to dispose of your trash correctly
- ꙮ Study the town plan

Chapter 4

Safety and Sanity

One of the first jobs to do in your new home is to install, if not already in place: smoke detectors, fire extinguishers and carbon monoxide detectors.

Only purchase those that have been tested and approved by a nationally recognized fire testing laboratory such as the Underwriters Laboratories (UL) or Factory Mutual (FM), and carrying their label.

Smoke Detectors

If the requisite smoke detectors aren't in place, it's up to you to make sure you have enough units and they are mounted in the right places. There are two basic types of smoke detectors: ionization and photoelectric.

- Ionization detectors detect the invisible as well as the visible smoke particles passing through a sensor. When particles interrupt or reduce the electric current passing through the sensor, the alarm goes off.

- Photoelectric detectors only detect the larger smoke particles that block a beam of light inside the unit setting off the alarm.

How smoke detectors work

Units are either battery-operated or electric (hard-wired), running off the house electric supply. Either should work. Although a combination of both is better. For example, one evening, a friend cooking fried chicken set off her

Heads Up When it comes to insuring your family's safety, not much beats having the proper detection and prevention equipment *in working order.*

electric smoke alarm system. Annoyed by the racket, she turned off the master switch, in effect turning off all three units in her house (one on each floor). She forgot to turn the switch back on after dinner. That night their wood furnace belched smoke up the staircase and into the bedrooms three stories above. Fortunately for the family, a pet woke them up in time and the actual fire was contained by their furnace, but just barely.

> There have been times when my cooking efforts have set off our multitude of alarms, sending the family running for towels and magazines to blow the smoke out of the alarms. At least they work!

Installation notes

When you install alarms, think of the path the smoke would take to get anywhere. Therefore, alarms should be installed in front of bedrooms in the center of the ceiling and not any closer than six inches (6") from where the ceiling and wall meet (where the air is considered "dead" or not moving), or installed at the lip of a ceiling at the bottom of a stairwell. In a multi-story building, install at least one alarm per floor as well as outside bedrooms.

Either type of detector, as long as the batteries are working, will give you and your family enough time to get out of the house. However, they are only as reliable as your maintenance schedule. If the batteries in a battery-operated unit are dead, the detector is useless. If the power goes out, any electric-powered units are useless.

We have units outside the upstairs bedrooms, just above each of the two woodstoves, on the ceiling at the bottom of the stairs, as well as inside the downstairs bedroom.

> The "fun" part of smoke detectors is when the batteries die unexpectedly, making a peeping sound every 30 seconds. Without fail, it happens at night. Trying to locate which one is peeping in the middle of the night is a trial! Keep plenty of 9-volt batteries around, just in case.

Warning

The most important criteria for installation of smoke detectors and alarms, is to *follow the exact instructions* that come with every unit.

Period!

In fact

Kidde recommends you change the batteries *twice* a year. At the very least—test the batteries themselves, as well as the detectors.

Are they working?

Once a month, test all the units by pushing the test button. Once, even better, twice a year, without fail, replace the batteries with fresh ones.

Not only do you know your units are in working order, but you won't have to deal with peeping detectors at weird hours.

Pick an anniversary, holiday, or birthday as the one day a year to make sure the batteries are changed and the units cleaned of dust. Another suggestion, when the clocks are set back or forward for Daylight Savings Time, change the batteries and check the alarms.

Fire Extinguishers

Fires are rated by the type of combustible feeding the fire. Extinguishers are rated by the type of fire they can extinguish. Not all extinguishers can be used on all fires.

Kidde Safety's website has pertinent information concerning fire safety. As a new homeowner, it is worth a visit. If you have children, the U.S. Fire Administration has a website with interactive games and teaching tools for children: www.usfa.dhs.gov/kids/flash.shtm.

The three types of fires are classified as:

- ❧ Class A-fires of ordinary combustibles or fibrous materials, such as wood, paper, cloth, rubber and some plastics.

- ❧ Class B-fires of flammable or combustible liquids such as gasoline, kerosene, paint, paint thinners and propane.

- ❧ Class C-fires of energized electrical equipment, such as appliances, switches, panel boxes and power tools.

Fire extinguishers are classified by the size and class of the fire they are designed to extinguish, and by their extinguishing agent. The higher the rating or classification, the greater the extinguishing capacity. For example, a unit

A Note From Kidde

As this information is so important, and they wish to disperse it as widely as possible, we are including Kidde's words concerning fire extinguishers and their use, with their permission.

Where Do They Go?

Not near a fire source, according to one firefighter, as that will be the hardest place to access the unit during a fire.

Once Used

Once the extinguisher has been used—if it is a rechargeable one, then get it recharged. If it is a one-time-use only, heave it in the trash—after discharging the entire unit. You can tell the difference between the one-time use and the rechargeable: the one-timers have plastic tops and handles, the reusables use metal for the tops and handles.

classified 4A can be expected to extinguish twice as much class A fire as one classified 2A. Some extinguishers are able to put out more than one class of fire and are marked with multiple ratings such as AB, BC and ABC.

Class A and B extinguishers carry numerical ratings to indicate how large a fire can safely be put out with that extinguisher.

Class C extinguishers only have a letter rating to indicate that the extinguishing agent will not conduct electrical current. Class C extinguishers automatically also carry a Class A or B rating.

ABC-rated multipurpose dry powder extinguishers are almost always red in color and have either a long narrow hose or just a short nozzle. These extinguishers are very light (5–25 lbs. total weight).

Check the pressure gauge on the fire extinguisher monthly—it must be in the green area (100 to 175 lb pressure) to work properly. Also, in dry chemical extinguishers the powder has a tendency to settle. Shake the extinguisher periodically to aid its performance.

Kidde advises homeowners to have one extinguisher for every 600 square feet of living space. They should be accessible on every floor of the house, including bedrooms, stairways, kitchens, basements, garages and have an extinguisher in every car or motorized boat.

> We have a small ABC extinguisher next to each bedroom door, another large one at the top of the stairs ready to grab if we need to beat our way to the front door, an extinguisher designed for use with electronic equipment in my office, as well as a special kitchen version handy to the stove. That's not counting the one in the basement area.

Fire Escapes

The higher the floor, the greater the need for something to get down. There are window ladders that can be kept near a window, in each room. Everyone has to learn how to open the box, attach the ladder to the window sill and drop it outside.

√ You want a ladder that stands out from the wall, allowing you to get your foot onto the rungs.

√ You want non-slip rungs. It must hold several hundred pounds of weight at once—enough for at least two people.

√ If there are young children in the household, can they get down it and use it?

√ Where is it stored? What is it stored in? How easy is it to use?

The pros suggestion is to keep the ladder under a bed, or other place, easily reached by the potential ladder user. Everyone should know how to use it—practice hooking the ladder to the window and throwing the ladder out the window so the braces are against the wall. Then practice going down the ladder. The last thing you want is someone to freeze in fright as they try to escape a burning building.

You might consider installing a special ladder on the side of the house. Jomy makes a great ladder that hides in a channel and looks like a drainpipe until the release at the top is pulled. The ladder and safety rail then drop down into place making a surefooted escape route to the ground.

CO Detectors

What doesn't stink, can't be seen and kills people? Too many people every year? Carbon monoxide.

Carbon monoxide is a deadly, silent killer. When CO is breathed in, it combines with the hemoglobin in your bloodstream (the oxygen-carrying agent in red blood cells) to form carboxyhemoglobin or COHb. If the concentrations of CO are high, you can die fairly quickly. If the CO concentrations are small, it takes longer—perhaps giving you enough time to get out of the situation.

Heads Up!
A young child may have a problem with this. Then you have to get out the window and down a shaky, wiggly ladder that doesn't always offer a great foothold. As there are many different types of ladders, don't settle for the first one you see.

The caveat here is that CO poisoning makes you dizzy, weak, sleepy, confused, sick to your stomach, headachy—and then kills you. The more CO in the air, the worse the symptoms, the faster it kills you.

Warning
After you get out to fresh, clean air, it then takes a while to replace the CO in your bloodstream with real oxygen again.

Any source of combustion can be a source of CO poisoning: kerosene stoves, gas stoves and appliances, woodstoves, fireplaces, chimneys, and the like—if they aren't working correctly or their vents are blocked. Cars running in garages, blocked chimneys or flues, back drafts from fireplaces or woodstoves can send CO into your house.

To be safe, install CO detectors that are UL 2034 listed. The Consumer Product Safety Commission recommends that "every residence with fuel-burning appliances be equipped with at least one UL-listed CO detector." There are plug-in and cartridge models. Follow the installation directions to the letter. Even better, have them installed by a professional. Ask your gas company or fire department what they recommend or if they can do it for you.

If one of these goes off, don't hesitate—*get everyone out of the house immediately!* If you aren't living alone, have a plan ahead of time as to where to meet outside or go to a trusted neighbor's house until the danger has passed.

Once you are out, call 911, the fire department or gas company to have someone trained check on your situation.

Radon Tests

Another silent, insidious killer is radon, an extremely toxic, odorless radioactive gas and extreme danger to your health. It is estimated that another 15,000 to 22,000 cases of lung cancer are caused, each year, by radon. It is the second leading cause of lung cancer, after smoking. To make this more exciting, the word "radon" comes from radium—i.e., it is radioactive. It is created by the breakdown of uranium. Any radon level over 4 picocuries per liter (pCi/L) is considered dangerous. Even that level can put you at risk.

The sources of radon are all around you: the earth, the rock beneath your home (especially that dumped and left behind by glaciers a few gazillion years ago), well water and not surprisingly but rarely, the building materials themselves. If there is radon present in the soil and rock beneath your house, the negative pressure in your house acts as a vacuum sucking the radon inside. If radon is in your well water, it can come through the pipes into your showers, and faucets.

Warning
Some detectors don't work well. We had one brand that was notorious for clamoring when there wasn't any danger. Make sure the brand you get is reliable!

The Iowa Radon Lung Cancer Study, conducted by Drs. R. William Field, Charles F. Lynch and colleagues found that there is a direct correlation between increased levels of radon and increased cases of lung cancer. In other words, the higher the radon, the higher the lung cancer rates. You can get far more information on the subject by going online or calling the National Safety Council at (800) SOS-RADON. There are several publications you can order from the EPA if you need to go into this further. One is the *Consumer's Guide to Radon Reduction*, another the *Home Buyer's and Seller's Guide to Radon*.

Kits can be purchased from hardware stores, online, your state radon office, and elsewhere, to test your radon levels. The cost is about $6–$20 per test including the return postage and lab work. The National Safety Council has a purchasing site online. There are short-term tests (about 2–4 days duration) and long-term tests (covering 90 days to one year). Again, follow the instructions to the letter, then turn the kit into the testing lab for analysis immediately.

If your short-term test comes in high, retest another short-term test immediately to confirm the results, meanwhile call on your state radon office for help. If the test is "iffy" try a long-term test too. One expert recommends using only the long-term tests as radon levels fluctuate greatly depending on other factors including weather—cold weather versus warm weather when windows are open more often, air conditioning use, and so on.

Testing is so simple, you might forget you are doing it. Simply put the test container somewhere in a lower or

Heads Up
The study was done in Iowa for a variety of control reasons—as well as the fact that Iowa has the highest radon levels in the country.

lowest level room in your house in a quiet corner, leaving the windows and doors shut. You can still use the room, please do so, but don't run fans or create drafts to clear the air. It defeats the test. After the prescribed hours or days have elapsed, find the container, pack it in the provided box and send it to the lab.

If you find that you have too high a level of radon, have your home fixed as soon as possible. The average cost to rehabilitate a home is $500–$2,500. Contact your state's radon office. They are usually found under the Department of Health and related services. They can advise you as to what is best for your location.

If you have purchased a home with a radon reduction system, find out exactly how the system is handled, and what is required of you for maintenance.

Child-proof

Obviously, if children don't live in your home, or visit often, skip this section altogether. If there are children in your family, this is vital information. It is *not* intended as the bible of children's home safety, simply checking safety issues that you may not realize are, or can be, problems in a home.

Medicine availability

Experts recommend that medicines be placed up high for safety's sake; in a cool, dark place for the medicine's sake. Locating anything medical, out of reach of small children, is the minimum safety precaution. Even a door catch or child's safety lock won't keep some children out of harm's way.

You might wish to keep a small bottle of Ipecac syrup available in case of emergencies—to be used under the direction of the Poison Control Center. Each poison control center has a non-emergency number. If you have children, call them or speak with your doctor about what to keep in an emergency kit at your house.

Wiring problems

Covers for electric receptacles are available in hardware stores and drugstores, and anywhere else baby items are sold. They are very common indeed. There are flat ones that plug in and cover the socket, and there are others that cover the existing plugs as well as the entire receptacle. These little items are cheap insurance! Both for your child, and your expensive electronics and other electrical appliances.

Office equipment

Paper shredders: these can shred the tips of little fingers, so turn them off when not being used. Better yet, unplug them if you have small children in the house.

Scissors left on tables or desktops can be a hazard, as well as Exacto knives and other sharp objects.

Check equipment wiring for any loose or frayed wires and keep it out of reach.

Kitchens and Bathrooms

Put away anything on a countertop that can be hazardous to children. That includes tweezers, knives, razors, pills, files and the like.

Ground Fault Circuit Interrupter

If Ground Fault Circuit Interrupter (GFCI) receptacles aren't installed in your bathroom and kitchen or other wet areas of the house, you should seriously consider having those installed—or installing them yourself. They can be purchased at any hardware store and run about $10–$20 each. Quite simply, they work like this: suppose you are washing your undies in the bathroom sink as you dry your hair. If the hair dryer drops into the wash water you can electrocute yourself. With a GFCI installed, as soon as the GFCI realizes there is a surge of power, it shuts off that electric line, effectively shutting off power to the appliance. The power stays off that line until you reset the GFCI.

Rx Alert
Even better, put a real lock on the door of the cabinet, or keep the medicines locked in another cabinet within a high one.

GFCI
The current codes call for GFCIs to be installed in all garages and outdoor installations.

Make sure you buy the same amperage GFCI as the switch you are replacing! These usually come in 15 or 20 amps and the rating is listed on the side of the switches.

Another way to check this is to check the main switch at your circuit breaker box. Those are rated by amps as well.

GFCI cover

Electric tester

When the light at the tip of the tester glows, power is coming through the receptacle.

To install a GFCI—first shut off the breaker at the circuit breaker or remove the fuse to that particular electric line. Test the line, preferably with a line tester from your electrical goodie collection (see the list of tools to keep around the house) or by plugging a light into the receptacle and turning it on, to make sure you got the right breaker! Unscrew the faceplate of the receptacle already there. Unscrew and pull out the old receptacle and look carefully at where the lines are shoved into the back of the receptacle, or wrapped around fat little screws. You want to match those exactly when you replace the unit. So, the best way to do it is to undo one wire and attach it to the same screw on the GFCI—the lines and screws are color-coded—until all three are done. Then squash the GFCI receptacle back into the wall box, screw it in place with the provided screws, and replace the cover and screw that in place. (Don't forget to turn the breaker back on.)

Warning

Lead paint is a hazardous material. *Don't you even think of removing it yourself. Have it done professionally.*

Lead paint

Lead paint is a dangerous poisoner of children. In houses and structures painted before 1978, when lead paint was banned, there is a danger that lead paint still exists. When you buy your house, if it was built before 1978, you should receive a certificate stating that the house is or is not lead free. If it isn't lead free, the lead must be safely removed or encapsulated.

Locks

Get child-proof cabinet locks for your kitchen and bathroom floor cabinets—and make sure they are the type that your children can't open. Then install them correctly. Do so for the drawers as well as the cabinets.

Perhaps you can save one drawer that is just for the children—sort of "their" kitchen drawer. Fill it with safe things to play with: toy cookie cutters (not sharp ones), measuring spoons, wooden spoons, little bowls. My kids loved to "bake cookies" with me and their supplies were kept in a drawer they could access anytime.

Get down on your knees and play kid

When's the last time you slithered along the floor? Much less got a floor's eye view of your home? It is a totally different perspective. To a small child, that is the view they have, and what seems safe to you looking down from above, may not be safe at all. Perhaps you can't see their access to electric cords and sockets, or other dangerous little things kids can and do swallow or poke at or pull.

Try to match the height of your child, or children, when you crawl around. Crawl with your child and make a game of it—as long as the child isn't going to get any ideas from your preventative actions. Look for tiny swallowable items, easy to pull out cabinet drawers, loose threads from furniture, window blind cords hanging too long and/or looped and dangerous. Don't forget the lovely china vases that could be toppled over. Think kid! Then correct the situation.

On the Outside

Nothing is better for children's safety than a responsible adult watching over them like the proverbial hawk. However, children have a habit of doing things we don't expect—such as wandering off when your back is turned.

Pools

Pools should have a fence completely surrounding them, high enough to keep children and pets out when they aren't invited. However, this plan is easily defeated by pools next to a house as part of a patio. Therefore, something else is needed to protect children. One idea

Instant Stairs

More than one little tyke has used drawers pulled out to form a staircase to climb onto the kitchen counter.

Window Blind Cord Warning

If you have small children, you want to make sure the cord doesn't make a loop that can strangle a child. Contact the blind company for a kit to finish off the cord ends.

is a plastic cover held up by floating balls underneath the covering, so it doesn't collect water that can drown a child. Your pool pros should have all the equipment you need to safety-proof your pool.

Hot Tubs, Spas

Plan for it
To be on the safe side, have some plan to protect your children from the hazards of the outside.

When not in use, cover the hot tubs and spas. Make sure the covering is one a child can't remove. I know, most weigh a small ton anyway…but some kids are pretty resourceful! Make sure any electric lines or plugs are not within kid's reach, if yours isn't a built-in unit.

Playgrounds and Equipment

As I remember from my childhood, my brother and I had a habit of "bailing out" of the swings. We just thought that was too cool. Mind you, he did knock himself unconscious on a hidden rock when he was 4 years old. So, make sure that there aren't any obstacles around any play equipment in your yard, or where your child plays.

There is a product made from shredded rubber that is excellent for playgrounds and other places where mulch is used. Rubber Mulch also comes in colors as well. It is more expensive than buying bags of mulch initially, but it doesn't have to be replaced. And the safety factor alone makes it attractive. (www.rubbermulch.com)

Chapter 5

Beat Catastrophe, Insure It

No one believes that nasty things will happen to them, but they do, so insure yourself for as much as you can bear.

If you never need it, you are one of the lucky ones. If you do need it, you will be forever grateful that you took the time to get the best coverage you could.

Wisdom
Insurance can rescue you, but only if you have it.

If you didn't get enough of the right coverage, who's to blame? Probably only yourself. Do it right the first time.

What types do you need?

There is more to homeowner's insurance than just insuring the house itself. If you have a mortgage, you must insure your home, for the benefit of the mortgage lender—not just you. Or the lender will do it for you at much greater expense than you can do it yourself.

You need to cover personal liability (someone gets hurt on your property and you are to blame, or will be blamed anyway), the contents of your house (clothing, furniture, jewelry, computers, toys, etc.), outside buildings (sheds, garages, etc.), home office, and your property when you travel. There are a lot of things to consider here.

If you have just purchased your home, was insurance included as part of your mortgage? If so, then this part may be taken care of—but is property damage included? Your contents? Liability? Check with your mortgage lender!

How Do You Get Insurance?

Do you go the route of using an agent? Or should you use the mail-in or online method? That depends on you.

Agents

Don't assume that every agent or insurance office is the same. They aren't. Shop around, see what is available. Make an appointment with the agent and get a feel for what that person is like and if you will get along.

I have an agent I trust implicitly. I wouldn't trade her or her staff for the world. They keep an eye out for our home, our business, as well as our children's interests when they get their own cars and apartments. In fact, we refinanced our car loans through her office and got even better rates than we did at the dealership. And our dealer was very, very low.

Of course, an agent can go overboard with trying to sell you insurance you may not need, so use your instincts, know in advance what you wish or need to insure.

Mail-In or Online

If you prefer the "mail-in" or online method, that's fine. Make sure that you are quite clear about exactly what you are having insured because if you aren't explicit the insurance company can come back at you and say "that ain't so, you're not covered." Compare policies!

The caveat here is—is there anyone to discuss your needs with? And how will they handle claims? If you prefer the personal touch—go with an agent.

Do your research

Before you pick an insurance company, check with your state's Insurance office (look in the white pages under your state's listings) to make sure they are quite legitimate and have a good record in dealing with claims.

A Word to the Wise

According to one insurance industry estimate, "70 percent of American homes are under-insured, by an average of 35 percent."

The New Protection Game, *Consumer Reports*, January 1999

Catch 22

Check to see which companies actually *pay* their claims. Don't forget the lessons learned from the hurricane season of 2005—Katrina and Rita. Many insurance companies got out of paying claims by citing damage from other than what the insured could prove. No matter which way the claim was made, the insurance company said the homeowner wasn't covered. It held up in court.

Get these questions answered:

- Are there complaints against the company?

- What is the rate of consumer satisfaction with the company?

- How does the company handle small claims? Painfully slow? Or quickly and efficiently?

- Does the company keep you informed of policy changes? Or ways to save money?

- Are there discounts on multi-*line* policies—having more than one type of policy with the same company (i.e., vehicles, house, business)?

- Are there discounts on safety features such as plenty of working fire extinguishers and smoke detectors, sprinkler systems or burglar alarms?

- Are there limitations on coverage? Does their policy cap the replacement-cost coverage? What about during a recovery period from a loss? Is there a set percentage that they won't exceed if you need temporary housing and reconstruction drags on?

- Are there special features in a policy that are attractive to you?

- Is the company financially sound? Can they stand a major loss? This is critical if you live in an area prone to natural disasters such as hurricanes, wildfires, tornadoes, or perhaps mudslides where many homes can be wiped out at once. Hurricane Andrew was a huge test for insurance companies. And many did not pass the test.

It Pays If—

If you are quite happy with your current insurance company, stay with it. Many companies reward long-term policies with discounts and non-cancellation clauses.

Really technical sources

More sources of information on underwriters (insurance companies) are insurance-rating services. This information can be found at public libraries, through The Insurance News Network's website, or through insurance agents. See Resources Appendix.

Warning
Be advised that all but Weiss Ratings charge the insurance companies to be rated. *Therefore, an insurance company can remove itself from a rating or listing if it is uncomfortable with the results.*

There were four major insurance rating services, but as there have been some serious issues with the companies involved (see sidebar), it is better to get the information from other sources now, such as *Consumer Reports*.

Lately, whether or not you get house insurance could be determined by your CLUE (Comprehensive Loss Underwriting Exchange) report. Essentially, this is a database compiled by insurance companies of all claims.

The insurance companies use the database records to calculate their risk as it pertains to your house. Unfortunately, while you may not have had any claims on this house, previous owners *may* have had claims—even if it wasn't paid by the insurance company, but by the homeowner, and reported to the insurance company as a "just in case"—and these would count against your home's insurability.

Only the owner of the property can purchase this report. It is available online as well. If there are any errors on the report, you, the owner, can have your side of the incident included in the report.

So, just like your credit report—you may need to keep track of your CLUE report.

Down and dirty quick answers

As to consumer satisfaction and other issues, one of the best places to find this information, aside from the rating services, is to check with *Consumer Reports*. If your library subscribes, and many do, check in their back issues. Even better, subscribe yourself. Or, subscribe to their online service, *Consumer Reports Online*, for the past several years worth of back issues as well as the latest one. As a new homeowner, you will find their information invaluable now and in the future.

Check around—Get quotes!

Don't be afraid of contacting many agents and getting quotes for coverage. You may be surprised at the differences between them. Compare the policies carefully before choosing one or two, then visit the agents, or have them visit you. Go with the agent you are most comfortable with.

There are plenty of online insurance comparison sites. Use them to get an idea, or range of the various companies, then pick the best company, even if their quote is reasonably higher.

Do-It List

Before you get quotes and make your inquiries, have this information ready to offer—this is all pertinent stuff:

√ What kind of roofing material is used—clay tile, shingle, wood shake, slate?

√ What kind of foundation—wood, concrete, block, slab, crawlspace, finished basement?

√ What kind of siding—vinyl, wood, asphalt, shingle?

√ What kind of interior wall covering—wallboard, plaster, fancy plaster or woodwork?

√ Age of your heating and cooling systems

√ Cabinets in kitchen and bathroom? Expensive or average quality? Expensive countertops?

Expensive appliances? Hot tub or whirlpool?

√ Extra windows? Skylights? Sunrooms?

√ Fireplaces?

√ Woodstoves?

Compare
When a young man complained to me that his insurance seemed excessively high, I suggested he go to an online site to compare his current rates with other companies. He was quite surprised to find that his policy cost was quite within the norm.

Types of Insurance

Personal Liability-Homeowner's Protection

It isn't just your home that is at risk. If a person is injured on your property, whether it is your fault or not, that could be covered under liability insurance. Suppose a neighbor's child falls out of your swing-set and is injured, or someone slips on your sidewalk and breaks a hip. If the injured parties are the suing kind, and you don't have liability coverage, you pay the damages out of your own pocket for any claims. Liability insurance covers these situations.

If you ever hire a contractor to work on your property, request a copy of their Certificate of Insurance before signing a contract. If the contractor can't produce the necessary Certificate, find another contractor who can. Many times the lowest bidding contractor is the lowest because the company doesn't carry insurance, expecting you to do so. This is not the homeowner's responsibility, nor is it fair to the other contractors who do pay for the necessary insurance. By law, all contractors must carry liability insurance.

Generally, $100,000 to $300,000 is considered a normal amount of coverage. If you have assets you wish to protect, get an *umbrella* policy. Depending on your circumstances, up to $1 million coverage isn't too much. This insurance is easy enough to add to a policy and should be included.

Medical Payments

This insurance covers the actual medical payments of someone injured on your property. If that child breaks a leg leaping off your swing set, medical payments pays the bills. The coverage limits are usually written as $1,000 per person per incident up to $25,000 for all persons injured in the same accident. Higher coverage is available, if you think you may need it.

Fair Warning

Suppose you hire someone to work on your property, perhaps a handyman or painter, and that person is injured while working for you. If the worker doesn't have insurance— you pay. One way to cover yourself is to only hire workers who have their own insurance policies and can prove it with a Certificate of Insurance from their insurance company.

Home—The structure itself

House insurance can cover just the minimum necessary for the mortgage lender to be happy, or all possible circumstances. Go for the best you can get. Don't think disasters can't happen to you. Even little incidents can be catastrophic—if you are not insured for them.

Your home can be insured for either its full replacement value or its actual cost. **Full replacement value** is how much would it cost to rebuild the *house* at the current building rates to exactly as it was before the catastrophe—not how much it cost to build, when it was built. If your house was built 10 years ago for $100,000 and it is now worth $140,000, but to rebuild it would cost $150,000—that's what you want to be insured for. Keep in mind that Full Replacement Value covers the house itself—not the land that goes with the house, as it usually isn't going anywhere. Therefore, the coverage is for the house and structures *attached* to it, such as garages or porches and decks.

Actual cost is the value of the item when built—not now. If it cost $100,000 to build the house 15 years ago, that's what you'll get to rebuild it now. Probably a far cry from its actual cost to rebuild it.

Outer buildings, not attached to the main house, such as separate garages, sheds, storage buildings—all not used in a business or rented to others, are covered for a limited amount in the policy. If you have an office or studio on your land used for business, not attached to the house, it should have its own policy.

Inflation Protection

Have your policy re-evaluated yearly to make sure you have enough coverage. Many policies automatically include an increase in premium to cover inflation. Known as *inflation protection*, this can save you the hassle of dealing with this.

A Word to the Wise

Keep an eye on the percent of increase in the value of your house. If the value seems way out of line, call your agent or company and ask them about it. Maybe you can get it reduced without adversely affecting your policy.

Four basic homeowner policies:

HO-2 The Broad Form covers fire and lightning, smoke, vandalism, theft, windstorms and hail, explosions, riots and civil commotion, damage by vehicles and aircraft, glass breakage, and volcanic eruptions, damage resulting from weight of snow, ice, sleet, surges or short circuits in electricity (radio and television tubes are usually not covered), or problems stemming from improperly functioning plumbing, heating, and air conditioning systems or domestic appliances.

HO-3 The Special Form (and one of the most common policies) provides all of the above, more extensive personal property coverage, and just about everything *but* damage resulting from floods, earthquakes, war, nuclear accidents and similar catastrophes.

HO-5 The Comprehensive Form provides the most extensive and comprehensive coverage available, but is not offered by all companies. If a company doesn't offer it, they may offer riders to the HO-3 to cover what is missing. Aside from war, earthquake, and flood, this policy just about covers everything. This can be the most cost-effective way to insure your home.

HO-8 Older Homes Policy which covers much older homes that would be prohibitively expensive to replace otherwise. This policy will only cover the Actual Cash or Market Value of the home, not what it would cost to replace. The actual cash or market value is what an appraisal says your house is worth on the market—*not* the cost to rebuild it. If, for example, you own a beautifully restored Victorian home that cost hundreds of thousands to restore, but the market value is only $300,000 after you spent the $500,000 to put it in that condition, you would only get $300,000 to rebuild the house.

An exception is the state of Texas which has only three policies it has approved: HO-A covers your home and possessions for *named* perils only, and just for the actual cash value; HO-B covers all perils, except those excluded,

Pay Attention

Earthquakes and floods are NOT covered by regular homeowners insurance. You have to get special insurance for those coverages.

for replacement value on the home, but actual cash value of the possessions; HO-C is more extensive than HO-B. However, their list of excluded perils includes flood, termites, damage from insects, mice, rats; earthquakes, wind or hail damage to trees and shrubs, losses if your house is vacant for 60 days or more.

Your best bet

You are probably better off getting the HO-5 Comprehensive Form, if available. The next best is the HO-3 policy, but this is between you and your agent and insurance company.

In Texas your best bet is the state recommended HO-B policy. There is an HO-A Amended that is somewhere between the HO-A and HO-B.

Warning Don't underestimate your need for property insurance.

Special Features

When you go to an agent, or apply for insurance, if there are special features as part of your house, such as expensive fixtures or cabinets, take a list with you or be prepared to offer a list of these features. Bringing those house plans with you would be a tremendous help. Even better, have your agent come to your house.

Other situations

If you are a renter or condo owner, there is insurance for you as well. HO-4 is renters insurance, HO-6 is for condo owners. All the rest applies as well—get the best insurance you can.

How to Value Your House

First of all, you need to know the square footage of the house. If you've just purchased the home, the real estate agent has that information handy. Or take the information off the house plans. With that information, call several custom builders and ask them what it costs, per square foot, to build a home. Then ask them the same question about building any out-buildings you have. It costs less to rebuild a garage than a house.

Now, multiply the Cost per Square Foot times the Square Footage of your home. Don't include land values here, as the land will still be there, as will the foundation (usually) after a loss. (Of course, mudslides are a different story and that is covered under flood insurance anyway.)

Fair Warning

Too many little claims on a low or no-deductible policy can flag your policy for cancellation or non-renewal. You must figure if this is worth the aggravation with a no deductible policy.

Figuring Replacement Coverage

Cost Per Square Foot _____

X Square Footage of the House _____

Equals: _____ $_____

For Out-buildings:

Cost Per Square Foot _____

X Square Footage of the buildings _____

Equals: _____ $_____

Subtotal (House + Outbuildings): $_____

Now, multiply this by 1.1 for "soft costs" or all the other things not included, such as architects fees, debris removal, permits, and other non-tangibles.

Total Insurance Coverage: $_____

With this chart in hand, you are ready to get policy estimates from several agents or companies. Don't be afraid to ask questions of the insurance company if you think the offered valuation of your home is too high. Almost 1 million of Allstate's California customers were overcharged for extra rooms or amenities their houses didn't have. The preliminary settlement of a class-action suit had Allstate agreeing to reimburse the customers as much as $120 million in excess premiums.

Don't allow the company to quote you less than 80% of the value of the house, either. If you do, you will receive only partial reimbursement of any partial loss leaving you with a huge bill on your hands. For example: you are only insured for 70% coverage and a tree crushes your garage, the bill comes to $10,000 to repair and rebuild. You may be stuck with at least $3,000 of the damage yourself.

If you make any improvements in or onto your house, have your policy re-evaluated immediately.

Deductibles-How much should you gamble

How much money do you have set aside to cover a loss? The deductible amount is the amount you pay before the insurance kicks in.

Deductibles start at none, then graduate to $100, $250, $500 up to a $1000 or more. The higher the deductible, the lower the insurance premium. If the insurance company doesn't have to pay for the little problems, it isn't shelling out money constantly and, therefore, will charge you less. For example: lightning strikes a tree in your yard and you are covered for that. The tree just blows apart (they do, trust me) and has to be removed. You get an estimate of $400 to cut down and remove the poor tree. If you have a deductible of $500, you pay the entire bill. The insurance company isn't bothered with any details. Although, you should report it just in case.

Suppose that lovely tree is struck by lightning and crashes through your roof. If you have a deductible of $500, and the bill comes to $8,000, you pay the first $500 and the insurance company pays the rest.

If you don't have that $500 for the deductible, or can't be bothered worrying about who deals with what, don't have a deductible. Then the insurance company pays the entire bill. It's your call. You have to know what you can afford out of pocket if something happens.

Personal Property

The contents of your house are insured as part of your homeowner's insurance. Depending on the company and your policy, the rate is 50% to 75% of the value of what the home is insured for. For example, if your house

Potential Savings

The higher the deductible, the lower the premium, up to 50% less with a $1,000 deductible. Insurance industry statistics show that the average homeowner files a claim once every 15 years.

You can save enough in those 15 years to repay yourself many times over.

is insured for $200,000, then your property is covered for up to $100,000 if you have 50% property coverage. Or $150,000 for a 75% coverage. Coverage is either at actual cash value or replacement cost basis.

Actual cash value means that the insurance company will only pay you what the item is worth, *depreciated*, at the time of loss. If your 10-year-old TV is stolen, and you bought it for $300, it would probably be worth only $50 today. That's all you'll get for it.

Replacement cost basis is how much it costs to replace the item in question. When lightning blasted our TVs, one set had to be replaced. Because we had Replacement Cost Basis, the entire cost of the new television was covered.

If you have gems, guns, furs and other valuable items, there are limits on what the company will pay if you suffer a loss. Document the value of all these items and get more coverage for them. The additional premium costs are worth it in the long run.

Inventory your household contents

This can't be stressed enough. As soon as you are moved in and organized, take pictures (color stills or perhaps video) of each room in the house, showing every wall, piece of furniture, special objects, art treasures, silverware, jewelry, everything. On the back of each photo write:

- what the object is,
- how much it cost to purchase,
- when and where it was purchased,
- if you have a receipt, where the receipt is kept,
- any other pertinent information.

Do this to anything of any value. Property worth over $200 will require "proof of ownership" meaning a receipt, warranty book, or a photo of the object.

If you have a total loss, the costs to replace your property add up quickly. The insurance company needs to know

Web Help

Most insurance companies have extensive websites where you can download or use their inventory sheets and get an idea of what they want you to prove about your possessions.

Inventory

Quicken financial software has an inventory system already built into their product. Look under Property & Debt.

what your property is worth to replace it. You need to know what to replace. After a disaster, personal or otherwise, you will be hard-put to remember anything, much less how many dishes you have, what silver service, how many curtains and so forth.

In addition, write all this information down and keep it in a safe place *away from your home*. Put it in a bank safety deposit box, or perhaps exchange copies of this information for safekeeping with a relative who doesn't live close to you.

Make a database or use a spreadsheet that comes with your computer to create your own inventory. Quicken® and other financial software programs have Home Inventory files to use as part of their Planning or Financial Records sections. Save the information to disk and store it off-site as well.

Combinations and discounts

If you choose one insurance company to handle all your coverage, rather than picking and choosing among the variety available, you may be eligible for discounts on all your insurance.

Buying insurance to cover your home and property, as well as your vehicles could give you discounts on all your policies. If your driving and insurance records are "clean," insuring more than one car can give you a multi-car discount. So it is with several policies with one company. You may or may not get a discount on your homeowner's policy, but you may also get a multi-*line* discount on your vehicles. Check with your insurance company to see what their discounts cover.

If you are a member of an organization such as AARP or AAA, they have group policies that may cost less.

If you are over 50 to 55 depending on the insurance company, you may qualify for senior discounts, as "seniors" or retired people tend to stay home more and therefore can spot a fire in the house more quickly. They also have more time to maintain their homes, therefore, a discount.

Need More?
If your house contents are worth more than what is offered, you can get more insurance coverage for your property. It will cost you more on top of the policy, but that is cheap replacement if you suffer a serious loss.

Important
All riders are based on "risk" or "exposure" of the issue in question.

If you have any questions about insurance companies, check with your state's Insurance Regulators. Look in the White Pages under your state's government listings.

The Extras aka Riders

Since insurance doesn't cover everything, such as earth-quake, flood, and computers in business, among others, you need "riders" to your policy to add this coverage. Riders are separate items of your choosing.

> "If you live in a high-risk area, one that is especially vulnerable to coastal storms, fires, or crime—and think you'll be forced to buy coverage from your state's high-risk insurance pool, check first with an insurance agent or company representative. You may find that you can still buy insurance at a lower price in the private insurance market than from the insurer of last resort."
>
> Insurance Information Institute, March 8, 1999

Flood

Think you may not need flood insurance? One in three flood insurance claims occurs in a "low risk" area. According to FEMA, the Federal Emergency Management Agency, every home should be covered by flood insurance. Even if you don't live near water. Hurricanes, overwhelming rainstorms and quick snowmelts cause devastating flooding, too.

Regular policies don't cover flood damage. How many thousands of homes were not covered by flood insurance when Hurricanes Katrina, Dennis and Rita hit in 2005? In 1968, Congress established the National Flood Insurance Program (NFIP) to help protect homeowners. The program is administered by the Federal Insurance Program under FEMA.

In 1983, FIP established the "Write Your Own" flood insurance policies allowing insurance companies to sell and service flood insurance. You can contact your own insurance agent and get a policy through their office, or

Do You Qualify?
If you live anywhere near a "body" of water, be it large or small, river or lake, or near the threat of water, have your location checked to see if it qualifies for flood insurance. If your community participates in the NFIP, you can get the insurance.

call the NFIP yourself at 1-888-CALL FLOOD, ext. 445 to find out where you can get the insurance.

There is a maximum of $250,000 worth of coverage through the NFIP, but there is insurance beyond that through your insurance agency with the first $250k as the deductible. None of this is inexpensive, unless, of course, you lose your home.

Yo, I live on a mountaintop!

Whatever—If you live on a mountaintop, you may not think you need flood insurance. But, if that mountaintop is actually geologically unstable ground, you live in a wet region, or receive serious amounts of rain, *get flood insurance. Mudslides are covered by flood insurance, not your homeowners insurance.*

If you live on or near a flood plain in a valley *near* a mountaintop, see if you can get the insurance anyway. Small creeks can quickly become flooded if a storm dumps more than a few inches of rainwater on them. It happens all the time. If the ground is saturated, the more likely that is to happen. When the ground can't absorb any more water, it runs off, down the creek bed into the river valley below. The water will come down in a wall sweeping everything before it.

One couple was refused flood insurance because their house was 25 feet above the little river meandering through our valley, and therefore, well above flood-stage. Within months, a devastating flood ripped through our valley with a wall of water surging through their first and second floors. Several nearby houses were simply swept away. Believe it or not, exactly two months later, to the date, it happened again.

Earthquake

Think you can ignore this section if you don't live in California? Think again. Even better, log into the U.S. Geological Survey's site on quakes and check out your state's history. While California may be on one of the

---

Assess your risk
The Floodsmart website has an interactive page where you can find out your flood risk, as well as figure out the premium. floodsmart.gov

There is a waiting period!
It takes a 30-day waiting period for the insurance to become effective, so don't waste any time thinking about it. Look into it now!

most active fault lines, there are plenty of others running through the continent.

In fact, the predictions are that somewhere in the United States a magnitude 8+ earthquake will occur. And it isn't necessarily in California. Memphis, Tennessee and St. Louis, Missouri are both very close to the New Madrid Fault in southeastern Missouri which experienced 8.4 and 8.7 quakes in 1811 and 1812. Those "little" quakes were felt as far away as Boston and stopped clocks in Charleston, South Carolina. Imagine the tremendous damage a quake would cause now.

For a paltry $.40 per year per thousand dollars of house value (excluding masonry veneer), we insured ourselves. That price includes a 2% deductible. If you have masonry veneer, the cost "rises" to $.65/$1,000. Therefore, if your home is insured for $100,000, you pay $40 for earthquake insurance excluding masonry veneer with 2% deductible. That is a bargain.

If you are a "gambler" with insurance, or not so sure, go for the 5% deductible without masonry veneer coverage.

Build-code Endorsement

This rider is especially important for older homes with wiring and plumbing that may not be up to current building codes. If your home suffers a loss and you must rebuild part of it, the building inspector may require you to upgrade your wiring and/or plumbing to the current codes. This endorsement will cover up to 10% of the insured value of your home to pay for the improvements. For example, if your home is worth $150,000, suffers a loss and must have a portion rebuilt, the policy will cover up to $15,000 for the re-wiring and plumbing work to bring the house up to code.

Backup of Sewers and Drains

Sewers and drains can and do freeze in the frigid northern climes. If the mess backs up into your house, you are in for a nasty cleanup. If something big lodges in your drain *outside* the house, it can cause a back up of your unwanted wastewater.

This rider is only good if caused by or resulting from water or sewage from *outside your plumbing system* forced into your house through your pipes or drains, or "enters into and overflows from within a sump pump, sump pump well, or other system designed to remove subsurface water which is drained from the foundation."

The coverage has a limit of $10,000 and only covers a "private residence on the residence premises" of the policy and only these personal property items:

- clothes washer and dryer
- food freezers and the contents (presumably food)
- refrigerators
- ranges
- portable dishwashers
- dehumidifiers

Small business/computers

Keep a computer in your house? Ask your agent or check your policy to see if your computer is covered under your homeowner's policy. Ask them if the computer is covered while traveling.

Desktop Computers

Many policies will automatically cover desktop computers and peripherals for up to $5,000 or so as part of the policy. You can increase this coverage up to $10,000 for an extra premium. If computer coverage isn't already part of the policy, it can be added.

Laptop and Portable Computers

If you have a laptop or portable computer, make sure you have a business policy to cover the extra exposure such a computer gets. Especially if the computer is often traveling with you. You may want to look into an insurance company that only deals with laptops and/or computers as they know and understand the risks and dangers involved in traveling with one.

Business Computers

If the computer is used in business, you should have a business policy for the computer. That policy should cover breakdown, replacement of your data, loss of income or the extra expense of renting replacement equipment to get you back up and running.

Insurance companies vary on how they handle laptops and the types of coverage offered. However, this is fairly standard:

The Big Howevers

"There is no coverage for other personal property. This coverage does not apply if the loss is caused by your negligence."

—From the State Farm endorsement

- If *you own a laptop and use it in your own business*, you need a business policy to cover the computer.

- If the company *you work for* owns the laptop, they must get the coverage.

- If *you* own the laptop computer, *you* must insure it.

Home Business

First of all, make sure your homeowner's insurance covers your business in your house, or on your property. If you have to get another rider, or policy—don't hesitate to do so. It could save your business! Talk to your agent before you run into problems.

Running a home business is enough of a challenge without worrying about "what if" something dreadful happens. What if your house is broken into and your computer stolen? And all your data taken with it? Make sure you have up-to-date backup data stored somewhere out of the house!

The "free" insurance here is plenty of up-to-date backups of all your data placed in a safe place *away* from your computer and home. If the data is stashed in your home, and the house burns down, even if the data is stored in a fire-proof safe, the heat will melt the disks or tapes. The fire won't burn the *paper* in the safe, maybe scorch it, but not burn it. However, it will be hot enough to compromise your data.

Do-It Now

Inventory your house contents, room by room, with date of purchase, price paid, and description. Photos of everything are even better.

Store a copy of your insurance policies in a safe-deposit box at your bank along with your inventory and proofs of purchase of high-ticket items.

Part II

Know Your House

Chapter 6

Water Works

Water is water. Yes? Well...now that you ask. Not necessarily. Some is drinkable, some isn't. You need to know the difference.

Just as plumbing is plumbing. Sure, go ahead and mix up the gas and water lines. Makes no difference—Right? *Wrong!*

Plumbing is piping of liquids throughout your home. Water lines carry water, other lines carry fuel: oil, gas, refrigerant and the like. Not to mention the lines that bring these liquids into your house through server lines.

Potable water

This is the water you drink. If it isn't potable, it isn't safe. City and town dwellers, as well as some village residents get their water from municipal water supplies. The safety of the water is the responsibility of the municipality delivering the water through the pipes to your house. It probably has fluoride added to ensure the health of your teeth, and in particular, children's teeth. Because of this, dentists don't do loads of drilling anymore, they've branched out into other fun things, i.e., braces, overbites, cleaning, destaining and other joys. To make this even more fun, in some places, you pay for the water coming into your house—as well as the water going *out* of your house.

Duct tape!
One of my friends found a small hole in her copper pipe spraying water all over her basement. She solved the problem, much to the hysterics of the local plumbers, by sticking a pushpin into the small hole, and wrapping the entire pipe and pin with wads of heavy-duty duct tape. The pin alone just didn't cut it—it kept blowing out of the hole.

Rural residents probably supply their own water via a spring or well. Deep drilled wells have a pump near the bottom of the well, shallow wells have a pump in the basement. From there the water is pumped into the house and into a pressure tank. Springs usually feed into a holding tank or concrete reservoir inside the basement, then the water goes through a jet pump into the pipe system.

City Water

Water provided by the municipality comes in from a huge feeder line generally running parallel to the street. From there comes the line to your house. The meter box is usually mounted on the basement wall with a remote "reader" outside convenient for the water meter reader to get to without disturbing you when the monthly rounds are made.

There should be a box buried just before the house with two main shutoff valves, one on either side of the meter. The one on the street side shuts off the water—completely, from the company, the one on the house side of the meter shuts off the water *after* it has been metered.

Turn it off, turn it on

You need to know exactly where that meter box is, and how to shut off the valves. Turn these valves *clockwise* to shut off all water to your house. If one of your big house pipes bursts, this is the best place to shut off the house water until that situation is cleared up. If it is a little pipe problem, it most probably can be taken care of by shutting off a smaller feeder pipe within the house. The street side shutoff valve is used by the company when they have to do work on the water pipes.

Wells and Springs

You should know the depth of your well, the depth of the pump, and whether the pump is fitted with a lightning arrestor. Believe me, they can be seriously deep down there. Ours is 510 feet down.

The way they work: a well-drilling company with special equipment comes to your location, picks a suitable spot—one that is safely away from any septic systems and within your boundaries—and drills the well until it hits water. The well is lined with metal pipe down to solid rock or bedrock. A pump with the water pipe attached is lowered down into the water. The whole thing is capped off, and the lines coming out of the well are run underground into the house. The well itself becomes a storage tank of sorts, with water rising almost to the top of the well.

You will find the electric fittings for the pump near the electric panel. There may or may not be a lightning arrestor alongside the fittings. It is a good idea to have lightning arrestors in the pump as well as the house. Our well has had too many direct hits and blown out too many arrestors to say you can't have enough of them!

> One winter our pump blew out. The well company pros came on a freezing January day and proceeded to pull up the pump. Every couple of feet the plastic pipe broke off. At first the pros said, "You don't need a couple of feet, do you?" When it got to 50 feet broken off, that conversation stopped. The entire 500 feet of pipe had to be replaced—and as the pipe was warrantied, the pipe manufacturer paid for the replacement.

The Right Way
The experts actually suggest breaking off the point of a lead pencil and wrapping the pipe and hole with duct tape until a proper fix can be made.

Tracing the lines

Inside the house, look for where the pipes enter the house. Find the concentration of equipment related to water, i.e., the water heater, perhaps a water softener, pressure tank (for well-supplied water), then trace back the lines to the entrance. Along the lines, you may find another shutoff valve, the globe valve, that also controls water pressure. It can be partially or completely shut down if necessary. Along an outside wall, you'll find a pipe leading outside to a hose bibb or outdoor faucet—the one to which you attach your garden hose.

Well-supplied water pipes could come up from the floor, while municipal water pipes could come out of the basement wall. At this point, it is one larger pipe, between ½ to one inch in diameter, coming into the house. Well-supplied water will first go into the pressure tank used to build enough pressure to push the water into the pipes up to the fixtures.

From there, the plumbing is the same. The water pipe splits with one line going into the hot water heater, then returning out as a hot water pipe running alongside the original cold water pipe to the rest of the house as needed.

The pipes running horizontally are called *runs* while the vertical pipes are called *risers*. Just before the pipes reach a fixture there will be a *stop valve* that can shut the water off to the fixture. From the stop valves come the *supply tubes* carrying the water to the fixture itself. For your own reference, locate each of these valves and see how they are turned off and on, via handles or knobs.

Water in your house pipes is under some serious pressure. Otherwise, it couldn't get up the risers into the fixtures. Which explains why pipes like to burst or spray….

My friend has used electrical tape and screw clamps on another section of her pipes. Here again, you can buy a pipe repair section in hardware store's plumbing sections. Until then, clamp a rubber hose over the hole using the clamps used for car hoses, or wrap a length of wire around the pipe and twist it tightly closed and repeat several times down the length of the repair.

Turning it on, turning it off

In an emergency situation the first place to go to stop a flood is to shut off the supply valve to the leaking fixture. Then you can deal with the fixture causing the problem. If the problem is in the line and not with a fixture, you'll have to go back farther down the line to the supply valve before the leak and close that down.

Too Cool!

The Gordon Tool Co. makes a dandy wrench just for turning on and off the shut-off valves under toilets and sinks. It is so simple, you wonder why no one else thought of it! Perfect for awkward places and smaller hands. If you can't find it in a store, call (949) 552-7613. Can't go wrong for under $10 with shipping.

If worse comes to worst, you'll have to go to the first valve allowing water into the house and shut that down.

Septic Systems

If you have a septic system, find out ahead of time what exactly comprises the system and where the components are located. When was the last time it was cleaned? If not overused (a constant houseful of guests abusing the shower or washer), septic systems only require a three-year or so pumping.

Septic systems work by using microbes to eat what is put down them. Normal household cleaners shouldn't be a problem. Don't overuse caustic chemicals to clean within the house nor pour them down the drain. It will kill those little microbes. Same with cute toilet paper: don't use the kind with scents or pictures, those chemicals kill our little friends. Plain white does quite well by itself. Hate to say it, but the same goes for those lady monthly-necessaries—they really don't belong down there. It is better *not* to add anything that says it "helps" septic systems, because they generally don't.

In many instances, the pipe running into the first big septic tank (the wet tank) isn't cut flush with the walls of the  tank, but left sticking out a few inches. Unfortunately, there is a baffle a few inches beyond that and wads of toilet paper can build up against the baffle and back into the pipe preventing what you just flushed from draining into the tank. At some point, it can back up into your house.

The lowest drain or toilet in the house will show the first effects of this problem. Whatever is flushed from above will revisit you in the bottom-most shower or toilet. Yuck!

Rural Rules

A rural rule of thumb is: If you didn't eat it or drink it first, it doesn't go down the toilet.

Clogged?

If only one drain is sluggish, try cleaning the gook from under the strainer or from under the drain plug. Shine a flashlight into the hole and see what you have to remove. Tweezers or a crochet hook work well.

If the toilets *and* drains get sluggish, time to check on getting the tank emptied, or having the drain pipes unclogged along the waste pipe.

Fertilizer!
We once planted tomatoes and potatoes over our leach field drainage. The end result was amazing. The potato vines were extremely long—and yielded one teensy potato! The tomato vines were about 14 feet long and really did yield loads of tomatoes.

In this situation, it's best to err on the safe side than not. If the situation is within the house and pipes, it is a plumber's job. If the situation is outside of the house, you need to check with the septic tank contractor or "honey wagon" companies. The honey wagon comes to your abode with very long lines that snake through the grass (or your house if it is in the way) to the top of your septic system. After the top is removed from your tank, the pipe is dropped into the tank, the contents are drained out, the tank is "backflushed" and repumped out leaving just a "starter" in the bottom of the tank.

What type is it?

There are several types of septic systems—dry and wet, chemical, mound and whatever else the engineers come up with. You need to know which type yours is and if it requires any maintenance. Chemical systems will require maintenance more than wet or dry systems as you control the chemicals, much like a swimming pool.

The most common septic system is the tank to leach field combination. Your waste drains into that tank downhill from your house, the microbes do their munching, the now partially treated effluent filters through another pipe to the leach field—a system of pipes full of holes that spreads the water around an area lower than the tank. That's where the "grass is greener" and you can get an idea of where your system ends. The water from the leach field filters through your dirt back into the great outdoors. This process takes months to accomplish naturally.

Dry wells are for non-bacteria-laden water, i.e., water from washing machines, showers and baths, or other fixtures that don't send possibly contaminated water out of the house. As washing machines can provide up to 40% of the water in the septic system, it is quite possible that your system has a dry well (meaning it isn't full of water all the time) to take on the wash water. Kitchen sink water, toilet offerings or dishwashers should never be drained into a dry well.

Does it comply with design codes?

This you should have found out when you bought the house. If it doesn't fit the current codes, you may end up having to upgrade the system to the tune of lots of money, if it fails. If the system is working just fine, thank you, and you know all there is to know about it—or you wish to know about it for now, relax. Just make sure it gets checked or pumped on a reasonable schedule. It's a good idea to know who to call when the time comes. Do your research ahead of time.

When was it last pumped?

This you should have found out when the house was inspected. If not, have the system checked anyway. The system, depending on usage, should be pumped every three years or so. If only one person is using it, then this can be stretched to a degree. But if yours is a household with children, you may wish to "follow the rule."

Where is it?

Knowing exactly where the system's components are is essential! Otherwise, when the time comes to pump the thing you may have to dig up the entire yard to find it. That is not a cool thing to do. Plays havoc with your landscaping. In fact, if you haven't done any landscaping yet, make sure you have access to the system and don't plant a huge tree on top of the main tank or leach field—because the green really is greener over there. However, a good septic company has the tools to locate the tanks without digging up anything. When the tank and access holes are found, then the dig commences. If the tank is deep, requiring a lot of digging, you might have a conduit with a cover put over the tank's cover to make it easier to access. It should come within a few inches of the level of the ground making future access quick and easy.

Shhhh! Years ago, a ski resort tried to use the water from the wastewater treatment system to make snow on their slopes. At this point the water is so pure you can drink it out of the last filtration tank. Well, that didn't go down too well with the populace! When that little idea broke out into the public it became a great bumper sticker "Where the Affluent Meet the Effluent" and the idea died.

Plumbing

What type?

Yeah, yeah, the type that carries water! Seriously, there are different types of piping. The old pipes, years ago, were made of lead. This is not good. If you haven't heard about lead poisoning, then read Chapter 4—Safety and Sanity. Then they went to copper pipes and galvanized metal, which are the norm these days. PVC pipes are used frequently as well since they are much easier to install. As of this writing, plastic pipes are used mostly for *returns*—the big pipes carrying away waste, outdoor plumbing, and perhaps some can be found under cabinets from DIY projects. You can find these gems in hardware stores everywhere. (They make great kids' play projects—soccer goals, for one.)

Have a look under the sinks, behind the toilet (usually a little silver pipe back there which is actually silver coated copper), and anywhere else plumbing or fixture pipes show. Find those little shut-off valves. That will give you an idea of what exactly you have and how to stop a flood. This is future reference material to be filed away until something goes wrong. Then you know how to sound intelligent when asked, "What kind of pipes do you have?"

Knowing what size pipes are used for what helps you understand what they are taking where. Drain or waste pipes are bigger than incoming water pipes. The main waste stack is usually a 4-inch pipe into which everything drains down into the municipal system, or your septic system. Incoming water pipes are about ¾ inch to 1 inch in diameter; within the house going to the fixtures pipes are usually ½ inch in diameter.

You may find a large pipe or two heading skyward as part of the waste stack, known as the atmospheric stack vent. That pipe allows noxious gases to escape the house safely, and to equalize the pressure in the pipe system, otherwise the pipes can bang or burst from the pressure.

When you look at the pipes underneath sinks, you'll notice there is a U shape to the pipe, known as a trap. That trap remains filled with water—also preventing gases from regurgitating back to haunt you. It does clean itself out every time you open the faucet above, and acts as a catch-all for things you think you lost when dropped down the drain (earrings, rings, etc.). To retrieve them you need the heavy-duty plumbing wrenches, a bowl for that bit of water, and some strength. It helps to have some plumber's putty to put around the threads when you put that lot back together again. The putty keeps the water from leaking out when you run water through the sink drain.

Tool Note
Sears has a clever new strap wrench for this little job.

Some traps have a little plug at the bottom designed just for this "lost ring" scenario. You still need that adjustable wrench or pliers (check which you need first) from your tool collection, a bowl and some strength. Be prepared for a bit of water to cascade down your arm when the cap comes loose. Your lost item should come with it. Make absolutely sure the plug is screwed back on as tight as you can get it, otherwise, you'll have another mess to clean up later.

Is it in Code?

All plumbing must meet a code of standards, although codes vary from state to state. The codes are designed to protect you, the homeowner, from poisonous gases returning back into the house, toilet water backing up into your tub, and other disgusting potential horrors.

It is the job of the plumbing contractor to make sure your pipes are up to code. If you do any work yourself, or have friends do some work, on your system, make sure what is done is within the codes. If it isn't, the results can be gross, hysterically funny, or possibly dangerous.

If a plumber or inspector finds that the plumbing isn't up to code, then the situation had better be rectified immediately. Have a qualified professional do the job.

Water testing

Take a sample of your water after sterilizing the faucet, sealing up the container, and mailing it back in. If there is a problem, the DOH will tell you what you need to do about fixing it.

Heat Tapes

Some brands of heat wraps are safe to use. Be absolutely sure that any you buy and use are UL approved. Follow the instructions for use to the letter!

Is it safe?

Back to the lead "thing" again. If your pipes are ancient, there's a rare chance they are lead. If so, have them replaced. Most likely there aren't any lead pipes around, as they haven't been used in many years. However, if you are renovating or living in a seriously geriatric home, it is a possibility. Returns of lead are not a problem, incoming water pipes would be.

Water tests can be done and should have been done before you purchased your house. That report should be with the paperwork you received at the closing and hopefully looked at before purchasing your house. If not, it is easy enough to have the water tested yourself. The first place to start looking for testing supplies or information is your own state's Department of Health (DOH). They are the watchdogs over the water supply, whether private or public. Check out their website, or call their office. They can direct you to the right office for help.

Water quality can change at any time. While your water may test perfectly on the day you buy the house, other factors change the water quality later. If you suspect a problem, get informed and get help—*now*.

Insulate pipes to protect from freezing

Those of you living in areas that deep freeze in the winter need to check your exposed pipes to see if there is any threat to those pipes. Look for pipes that are close to the outside of the house. Especially pipes in basements or along outside walls that are not insulated. You can insulate these yourself with kits of insulation from the hardware store. Pipe wraps are long black foam pieces with a slit down the side allowing you to slip the foam over the pipe. Use contractor-quality duct tape, if necessary, to secure the foam in place. Don't wrap it tightly as the foam is useless if squashed.

If you find that one pipe continuously freezes, look for *why* that pipe freezes. Check your insulation along the house sill plate (the part where the foundation meets the rest of the house) for holes and/or lack of insulation. There may be a hole to the outside exposing the pipe to freezing air. Block off the hole. If necessary, insulate around the area. You can buy cans of foam insulation that you spray into an area. The foam swells up to fill the void and insulate.

Water Heaters

There are as many sizes and shapes of water heaters as there are pipes. Tall, fat, squat, thin, tiny, gas, electric, tankless and I'm sure there are some I've missed. The typical gas and electric water heaters are comprised of a 20- to 80-gallon tank (normal is 40–80 gallons for a household) stuck somewhere convenient to the water supply, usually, but not always, in the basement. Water goes in one pipe from the water supply coming into the house, another pipe leads out to where the hot water is needed: kitchen, bathrooms, laundry area.

Common to all tank heaters, the well-insulated glass-lined unit, is a large cylindrical tank with tubes running into and out of it. Some tubes enter from the bottom, some from the top. Water comes in cold and leaves hot from the top. There will be a small faucet on the bottom to drain water out of the tank. Somewhere near the top will be a pressure relief valve—a safety device to prevent the tank from exploding if the pressure gets too much for it.

Gas

Natural gas is more prevalent as it is more widely available to most of the country. But propane and other "fired" heaters work the same way.

Gas heaters have a vent pipe that leads out from the top center of the unit to the outside of the house, whether through the wall, or up through the roof. Water flows down into the tank through a pipe that will have a shut-off valve just before it enters the tank. The cold water drops to the bottom of the tank, is heated by the burner located at the bottom underneath the tank itself.

Oops! If for some reason there isn't any water in the tank, make sure the unit is shut down—completely.

Remember You should have had your gas company pro explain all this when you bought the house.

Flames

Check the flame on your burners occasionally as the flame should be blue with perhaps the merest hint of yellow. If there is a lot of yellow in the flame, you need to have your unit serviced quickly.

Gas comes into the bottom of the unit through a thermostat and into that burner set underneath the water tank. When the temperature of the water gets too low, a pilot light fires the burners to raise the heat of the water to the temperature you set on the thermostat.

As you turn on hot water taps, the water is drawn out of the top of the tank into the pipes to your tap. Immediately, cold water comes into the tank to replace the hot water removed. The burner comes on to heat the new water. The tank should always have water in it, ready to use.

There is a large hole in the bottom of the tank at burner level where the pilot light is located. When the heater needs to have the pilot light relit, that's where you do it. *Follow the directions on the unit absolutely!* They are posted front and center. If in doubt, call your gas company to have someone light it and show you how to do it properly.

There is a shut-off valve for the gas before it enters the tank. You need to know to what all these valves feed fuel: the water heater, dryer, gas stove, etc., and how to shut them off.

You also need to know how to shut off the gas from the outside of the house, coming into the house. There should be a box or a valve near where the pipes come in. In an emergency, turn off the gas outside the house. To be really prepared, if a wrench is needed to shut off the gas, keep one in the box so you don't have to search for one under stress.

Water line IN
Note shut-off valve

Water line OUT

Gas line

Vent

Electric

The cold water is heated by two long U-shaped rods, called elements, inside the unit. One is located about 1/3 down from the top of the tank, the other about 1/3 of the way up from the bottom. There is no vent to an electric water heater, as there is nothing to vent out. An electric cable brings power to the unit to heat the two elements. Sometimes, these elements get grossly encrusted with calcium deposits from the water. If you are not interested in cleaning them off yourself (and who is!), have a pro come and replace them.

Tankless

Europeans have used these tankless water heaters for eons. It is the norm. Essentially, a tankless water heater provides hot water by passing tubes of water through a gas burner that heats the water literally "on demand." The tank will be close to where the water is used. When you turn on the tap, the unit fires up and hot water is at your service. As long as water is passing through the "fire" you have hot water for as long as you need it. Unlike electric water heaters which may take "forever" (depending on the size of the water heater and how much you are using), tankless heaters keep on going. Since you are only heating water when you need it and not for the times you aren't even at home, it saves you lots of money.

Off-the-boiler

There are still some boilers with water coils winding through them that provide your hot water supply. To have hot water all year long, the boiler must be on. This isn't always practical—especially in summer. This method can be used to preheat water for your hot water heater saving you money. Any repairs or maintenance would have to be performed by the pros who installed the system.

Cleaning and maintenance

It is suggested that once a year you drain a gallon of the water out of the bottom of the tank to clean out the sediment and debris. It makes the unit much more efficient.

Attach a garden hose to the drain faucet on the bottom of the tank and only drain a gallon through the hose into a bucket. You shouldn't have to turn off the tank if only draining a bit of water, as the water is replaced as you drain it out.

For gas, follow the instructions on the tank to the letter! If you don't know how to do this or have any questions, *call*

However Check the rules for the water heater temperature in your state, as new rules could be in effect. In Vermont, now, the minimum temperature is 140°F due to *possible* Legionnaire's Disease.

the gas company. Don't ever hesitate to do so. Screwing up on this can cause a nasty explosion.

Leasing or buying

Interesting discussion this. You may not have the option. Look on the appropriate bill for a rental charge for your heater. Ours was on the propane company's bill. If there is no charge, you probably own the water heater outright. End of discussion.

Smart—

Don't forget to consider Energy Efficient water heaters if you make a change.

We "rented" or leased our water heater for $11 a month. The advantage of leasing/renting is that the company that owns the water heater must maintain the water heater. If your heater dies on you, even on a Saturday night, they have to send someone out, at their expense, to fix it! If you own it, you pay that repair bill.

If you have a choice to make, take all this into consideration. However, figure the lifetime of the water heater. If you buy one and it is warranted for 10 years, figure that against what the gas company (if they do lease equipment anymore) charges.

Using our old bill as an example, we paid $11 for ten years or well over $1000 for a water heater that costs around $500. It was repaired once at their expense. And the leasing company replaces damaged or dead ones. But did we save money? No, not really.

Do It List

- Learn where all the valves to your fixtures are and how to shut them off
- Keep whatever tool is necessary to turn off a valve in an emergency, near the valve in full view
- Know where all the major pipes are coming into your house—as well as going out of the house
- Learn what systems you have attached to your pipes, what runs them and where the fuel or liquid comes from

Chapter 7

Staying Warm, Staying Cool

Warm and Cozy Systems

There are plenty of variations on heating systems, literally from the ground up. Heating is provided by basically gas, oil, electricity and occasionally coal or wood. The heat conveyance can be provided by steam, hot water, or electricity, or by hot air.

If you live in the northern, much colder parts of the country, by all means, try to have a backup heating system available in case of a power outage. Woodstoves are not uncommon in the countryside and do a much better job than a fireplace, which is pretty useless, as an alternative heat source. But you must have a very safe, well-constructed chimney to vent the stove. If you don't have a woodstove, consider installing one. Not only are they great heat sources, but you can cook on most of them as well.

Furnaces—Hot Air Systems

Furnaces heat air that is then circulated throughout the house through a metal duct system. Often known as a "forced-air" system, this is one of the most common methods of heating homes. The most common fuel is natural gas. Where natural gas isn't available, there is LP gas, oil, coal, wood or electric.

The house's cool air is drawn down to the furnace where it is heated in the heat exchanger. The warm air rises into the plenum (a large box on top of the furnace) where it branches off into the duct system to the rooms.

"Registers" are located throughout the house. These openings in the floor or wall have a grille over them with a lever on the side to close the grille. Each room will have at least one for incoming air, perhaps one for the cold air (return grille with no adjusting handle) to be circulated back to the furnace for reheating. The grilles must be kept open and clear of furniture, drapes and other obstructions if the system is to work properly. If the return grille isn't in the same room (sometimes there are large return grilles in halls or larger rooms), the doors are cut 1–1½" shorter to allow air to circulate. This works as long as the air can circulate over any carpets or other obstacles.

However, it is fairly easy to control the temperature of the air in each room. If a room close to the furnace gets overheated, close down the register allowing only a smaller percentage of the warm air to enter the room. By adjusting the grate's baffles on each register, you can even out the amount of heat getting to each room. It may take awhile to find a balance that suits you, but persistence pays off.

Maintenance

The company supplying the fuel should be the company to maintain the furnace. There are air filters that must be changed frequently, depending on the season and usage. That's simple enough. These can be purchased at hardware stores by the carton. Slip out the old one, slide in the new. If there are months between seasons in the more moderate climes, you can slack off on those months. Do have the fuel company inspect the system on a yearly basis. When you bought the house, you hopefully made contact with the company and learned about your system from them. If not, then contact them now and learn about your system and what you need to do to maintain it. If you follow their maintenance schedule, you will prolong the life of your furnace.

Energy-wise

Shut down the heat or close off any rooms that don't require normal room temperatures thereby saving the cost of heating those rooms.

Gas systems are generally so efficient that they don't need yearly check-ups. However, problems have occurred in the past, so follow your system pro's advice on this one.

Boilers

Boilers heat water in pipes passing through the boiler heating chambers. The warmed water is then circulated through pipes to radiators in each room. Fuel in the form of gas (piped in through meters) or oil (delivered by truck to a tank) is the norm, with coal and wood used where other fuels aren't readily available or if you have a multi-fuel appliance.

Radiant Heat

Radiant heat is done several ways. Lately, there has been great use of radiant heat in floors. Using water tubes laid in concrete slabs or within the structure of wooden floors (installed to the underside of the wooden floor between the joists), the hot water warms the floor first and anyone or anything on it. The heat radiates upwards. When installed properly (i.e., no holes were poked into the tubing during installation causing leaks, or no kinks in the tubes), this system is a warm-addict's dream.

Another form of radiant heat is from radiators. The old versions were heavy cast iron monoliths taking up a sizable piece of wall real estate. The modern versions are sleek, more efficient and almost not there. Some radiators are flat panels, about 4" high with tubes running through them, lining the perimeter of the room as baseboards. They all deliver the heat by radiating and convecting heat into the room while keeping the heat source (the water) sealed and circulating back to the boiler for reuse.

Maintenance should be done at least yearly by the fuel company to check on the boiler itself. If your boiler is oil fueled, maintenance is a yearly necessity as these appliances are quite dirty. Gas units are much cleaner.

Energy-wise

Throw another blanket on your bed, and turn down the heat in the bedroom. Actually, it's quite comfortable to sleep in a 64°F room at night with the right covers.

Smart trick

One way to make the older stand-up radiators more efficient is to line the wall behind it to reflect the heat back into the room. Even tinfoil does the trick.

Steam

Before 1950, it was quite common to have a steam heat system using radiators to heat a room. The boiler boiled water to about 160–180 degrees Fahrenheit until it turned to steam which raced its merry way around the building through the radiators, heating the radiators, which in turn heated the rooms. The old units are quite noisy rascals, those radiators—honking and wheezing. And the system didn't do a great job of evenly heating a home. Some rooms can be much warmer or colder than others. But, the boiler heated your water, saving you a water heater. Trouble was/is, you have to have the boiler on year-round to have hot water. Off-season if you shut the boiler down, a regular water heater could be used. Or perhaps the boiler is used to warm the water before it goes to the water heater, saving money.

Ah, Modern

The newer hydronic systems are more efficient and also heat your water.

The older systems aren't a very cost-efficient way to heat a house. And to top that, a house that old probably isn't well insulated, making it even more difficult to heat. However, replacing an old boiler system with a completely new system probably isn't cost effective either due to the cost of a new system's installation expense. Insulating the house is more cost-effective.

We lived the rural "dream," for a very short time, of running a ski lodge in the 1970s. Of course, the building was an old farmhouse with an ancient steam boiler and no insulation. The thermostat was in the back corner of the dining room and behind the steam pipes leading upstairs. This was not a good place to locate it. While 18 people were eating, naturally, the room warmed up nice and toasty—causing the thermostat to shut down the heat to the rest of the lodge. Just wonderful. Peter got crafty and pushed up the temperature to 90 degrees while we were eating. Since the dining room never got to 90, the rest of the lodge heated up quite well.

As old boilers generally use oil to burn, the boiler needs yearly maintenance in the form of cleaning—at the very least. Have the company providing the fuel check the boiler and maintain it, without fail, on a regular basis. Not having this done can be too dangerous to think about.

Propane

The more proper name for propane is Liquid Propane Gas or LPG. Propane heaters are used in more rural areas where piped in fuel just doesn't happen. There are plenty of excellent, efficient heaters that can heat large spaces with a small heater. The fuel is delivered to your tanks outside and a pipe is run underground into the house. See Chapter 2—Get Functional for more information on getting your tanks filled and scheduling refills.

You need to know where the gas pipe comes in, where it goes, as it probably goes to a water heater, and most importantly, how to turn the gas off. You also need to know how to read the gauge on the tank—just in case.

Maintenance can be as easy as vacuuming the filters when you vacuum your floors—about once a week during the heating season. A single button turns it off and on. You can vary the humidity in your home by adding water to the unit. Some units have thermostats built in that let you set a temperature rather than using a slider that lets you guess. The newest of these are extremely efficient heating systems. They are excellent for heating additions, remodeling projects and basements where it isn't cost-effective to continue the main heating system in the house. One thing you do need to know is where is the shut-off valve to the propane. There should be one on the unit itself as well as one along the line into the house.

As they come in various sizes and capacities for heating, if you are considering one, you need to know how many cubic feet you are heating. You also need to know how well insulated your house actually is.

Heads UP

If your heating system gets less efficient over the season, have it checked and/or cleaned.

For example, we have used one Rinnai 1100 to heat our entire upstairs, over 22,000 cubic feet, in Vermont where 0º–20ºF is the winter norm and it does get much colder. Our house is extremely well insulated with at least 8" in the walls, and 20" in the ceiling. We have 2 roof windows as well. Yet this little heater pumps out the heat quite well. We use a ceiling fan to help spread the heat around and when the temperatures drop way down, we use our wood stove as a boost.

Energy tip

Those cute little heater cubes used to heat up space quickly are actually super energy hogs.

Electric

Electric heat is another form of convection/radiant heat. Until the oil crisis of 1973, it was quite commonly used as electricity was cheap. For houses built off the main gas pipelines, it was definitely the way to go. Now, electric isn't "cheap" anymore.

The electric current is passed through radiators mounted along the wall, usually under windows, and the resistance heats up fins in the radiator, which heats the air passing through. An air current is created when the heated air rises pulling cold air through the bottom of the unit, heating it and so on.

There are radiant floors that are heated electrically too, using wires under tile floors. These can be more efficient than older radiators as many use 110 volts instead of the radiator's 220 volts—depending on the size of the floor being heated.

If you look at your circuit breaker, any electric radiators take up 2 little breaker switches "ganged" together, meaning a 220-volt line is going to each radiator. That's a powerful load of electric. To save money, turn off the radiators you are not using and turn down the thermostats on the ones that you are using.

Maintenance on these is very easy. Before you use them at the start of the heating season, for safety sake and your own sense of smell—vacuum them. The dust reeks when you turn them on. As the fins heat up, they burn off the dust accumulated over the summer. Make sure nothing is touching the radiator, or is too close to it. This is a fire hazard.

Woodstoves

There are many people in rural areas who use woodstoves as their primary heat source. It isn't always practical as many stoves need to be stoked frequently. There are newer models of stoves that need stoking only once a day. You still have to spend time getting the wood, stacking it, and then carting the stuff inside the house. Having done this for years, it is a time-consuming chore, but many times, when all is working as it should, quite a pleasant way to take a pause.

Pellet stoves These have become quite popular, increasing their price as well as putting such a demand on pellets that the price of those has gone up too.

If you use or plan to use a woodstove, watch out for creosote. That's the black stuff formed by incomplete combustion of the gases given off as the wood burns. The lower the temperature of the fire, the more creosote. If enough moisture is still in the wood, the chimney gets coated with a black glaze of creosote, Class 3—which can be deadly. It ignites and burns easily. If you notice this condition, buy a bottle of *Anti-Creo-Soot®* (ACS) from your hardware store, stove store or sweep and follow the directions. Essentially they are: while the wood and stove are cold or the embers are low, spray a few shots of ACS on the wood, then light the fire or stoke up the embers into a good fire. ACS is quite safe to use and very effective. Do that once or twice a day and your problem is just about solved. *The big however—this doesn't eliminate the need for a chimney sweep to clean the chimney frequently during the heating season as well as before the stove is first used each year.*

The pluses to wood heat are the comfort of a nice, toasty stove radiating warmth. The drawbacks are: getting the wood—whether paying a fortune now for the chopped and stacked wood or chopping and stacking it yourself, drying it—or rather allowing it to dry out so it burns better, carting it into the house, protecting your house from the bugs that inhabit the wood pile (by keeping it some distance from your house), uneven heat, having to stoke and reload the stove at least twice a day—which means you can't leave during a cold spell for any length of time. At least you get exercise!

Storing wood

Be careful where you store your wood. Too close to the house could make a great breeding ground for unwanted bugs. Better to store your wood away from the house, under cover.

Same goes for the basement or crawl space, or particularly a dirt cellar.

An old Vermonter offered this very effective way to dry out wood. It goes against most people's notions (including other Vermonters' ideas) on how to dry wood quickly. Stack up your wood pile in a sunny place and cover the entire stack with plastic. Cut 6" slashes along the top side edge of the plastic all around. It took a month for our several cords to dry out completely—instead of the usual months and months.

Heat Pumps

Believe it or not, heat pumps work by extracting heat energy from cool air, and cool from hot air, to heat and cool a building. It is essentially an air conditioner working both ways. There are several types of heat pumps: those that work using air or water extraction and those that work underground.

The air units are quite efficient until, of course, the temperature is really too cold for the system to work—at the freezing mark. When the pump can no longer extract warm air from the outside, it uses an internal electric heating coil for warmth. This can be expensive.

The ones using the ground for heat and cooling are quite efficient as the ground temperature, deep down, is fairly constant.

Saving money

Setback thermostats aren't new, but if you don't have one, installing one can save you a bundle. While 68–70°F is quite comfortable during the day, 62–64°F is quite comfortable at night. If necessary, throw on another blanket or use comforters. If no one is home during the day, set the thermostat to keep the house temperature down until about 30 minutes before anyone comes home and drop it again after everyone goes to bed.

Turn off and unplug appliances, computers, and other stuff that holds power. Think about it: you may use your computer only 8 hours a day if you work on it, leaving 16 hours a day for it to use power while not being used.

Turn off lamps when no one is in the room. Use the highly efficient compact fluorescent lamps (CFL) wherever possible. Many electric companies can help you with coupons to help pay for the bulbs. As they tend to last longer, the bulbs do pay for themselves in the long run.

More information on this subject is in Chapter 12—Energy Efficiency.

Energy Audits

Anyone, anywhere, can get an energy audit of their home. Check your power/utility company websites, the phone book, the little flyers sent with your power bills, call the power/utility company to ask. Check the websites listed in the Resources section.

Energy conservation pays big dividends to all of us over the long haul. Even if you live in the south, an energy audit should serve you well.

Have an energy audit done of your house. The audit will tell you if you have enough insulation (if you don't already know), where you might need caulking, whether or not an "invisible plastic" window will do your windows any good to keep out cold.

The "invisible plastic" window is a sheer plastic sheet that covers an entire window using double-sided tape to seal the plastic to the window frame. When installed properly using a hair dryer to tighten the plastic, you can't tell it's there. It effectively eliminates drafts through windows. You can buy it at your local hardware store. Cheap chill chasers. Chapter 12 has more on energy savings and audits.

Need help? Most energy companies, banks, or your state's Community Action Councils can point you low-cost loans to help weatherize your home.

Energy battle

Turn *off* the furnace, in *summer*; turn off the air-conditioner in winter. Don't have both running at the same time, or you'll have both units fighting each other constantly.

If the heat is set at 72°F for the winter, and the air-conditioning to 68°F for the summer—you have a problem.

Reverse those settings, you'll still be comfortable, and the energy and money saved is significant.

Keeping Cool and Calm

Although costly, air conditioning is essential in many parts of the country for maintaining the comfort of your home, especially when temperatures soar.

There are other ways of cooling buildings naturally, but modern architecture avoids tried and true technology. Until the 1950s and the advent of air conditioning, buildings were designed to stay cool in summer and warm in winter.

If you see pictures of houses in Germany, most, if not all of them, have big overhanging roofs. The reason is quite simple. As the sun is low in the winter, it can reach into the farthest corners of a room and heat it. In the summer, the angle on the roof is such that sun can't get into the building at all—and therefore can't heat it. Windows are smaller on the wind or north side of the house, and quite large on the southern, sunny side. Passive solar at work.

What kind is it?

Air conditioning is rather simple, if you have it. The system can be part of your central heating system, or a small independent unit for each room. If you have whole-house air conditioning, as part of your package, it works off the furnace's air circulation system. The condenser is usually located outside. The units stuck in windows are independent of anything but their electric plug. All air-conditioners are electric powered.

How does it work?

Warm air is pulled over copper evaporator coils filled with refrigerant, warming the refrigerant and cooling the air which goes back into the room or building. The warmed refrigerant is sent outside to the condenser where it loses its warmth to the outside air. Once cooled it is returned to continue its work. In whole-house systems, the condenser unit is a big vented metal box outside; the window units contain the condenser in the part that sticks out of the window.

Who maintains it

If your system is a combination heating/cooling system, the same company that installed it maintains it.

The window units are yours to maintain. You bought it, you maintain it. If it busts, get it repaired or get another one. Try to get the most energy efficient unit you can find. The more energy efficient, the cheaper it is to run—thereby saving you its cost in the long run.

The filter must be changed frequently in your air-conditioner. Find out the most effective schedule (i.e., monthly, weekly, etc.) and do it. Filters are available at hardware stores.

Other Cool Ways to Save

Add ceiling fans

One of the most cost-effective ways to cool a place is with ceiling fans. These are quite inexpensive to run at only pennies a day. We have one in every room upstairs as even Vermont gets quite hot in the summer. We have a powerful fan in our bedroom that we call the helicopter as it creates such a downdraft that we need covers even when it is 80 degrees outside at night.

Some fans are quite elegant with lights hanging below. Others are utilitarian. But they do their job very well indeed. If you get one, make sure it has at least three speeds. If it is to be mounted high up on a ceiling, make sure it has a remote control, or both the fan and lights can be controlled separately from the light switch.

Shades

When the temperature is supposed to get brutally hot, if you shut down the house by closing all the windows and doors before the temperature rises, and lower any shades on the sunny side of the house, you can spare yourself a cooked house. At least for a little while.

If you have a bit of an overhang, install little vinyl roll-up shades on the outside of the windows. They will keep

Energy-wise

Think about this one—if everyone in the sun states had solar power running their air-conditioning, there wouldn't be such a strain on the power grid. Any excess power could be sold back to the power company!

Seasonal Note

Don't forget to reverse the fans at the change of seasons. In summer you want the air to flow down to cool you, in the winter you want the air to be pulled up to recirculate.

Outside shades

These bamboo roll-up shades keep the summer sun from baking the inside of this house. They are rolled up on cloudy days allowing a view of the mountains beyond.

the sun out of the house altogether and you can keep the windows open if you need to. These shades are available wherever housewares are sold.

Don't forget awnings! Another great way to beat the sun. With these installed, you can keep the windows open and the breeze blowing while keeping out the sun.

Trees

Deciduous trees, strategically planted, can lower your heating/cooling costs all year. Deciduous trees are the ones that lose their leaves in the fall. In the spring, they leaf out creating tons of cool shade. In the winter, they drop their leaves and allow the sun to warm your house.

For example, we live in a little clearing in the woods. Our summer temperature is at least 10 degrees lower than the surrounding areas and in town. In the winter, I can usually keep my Impatiens growing outside until about November, while everyone else's are dead from the killer frosts of September and October. It does take a bit longer for our yard to green up come spring, but it is a small price to pay for the cooler house temperatures in the summer and the warmer, protected winters. We have a maple tree growing next to our deck that now shades the entire deck all summer.

If this idea is something you think will work for you, speak to a landscaper or nursery company and ask them about your place. Take them a drawing of your house in relation to the sun and yard. If this is a practical move, it could save you big bucks and increase your comfort through the years to come, as well as increase the value of your home.

Chapter 8

Electrical Systems

This section is rather easy. Electricity comes into your house from service lines along the street, either up in the air to an upper corner of your house, or through underground conduits. However the lines get into your house, nearby will be a circuit breaker box with a shut-off switch to the entire electrical system in the house. Also known as the "mains," the electricity is fed throughout the house first through breakers, akin to the shut-off valves in the water system (or in really old houses, a fusebox using fuses instead of breakers), then through the walls into receptacles or switches.

The Circuit Breaker Box

The circuit breaker box can be found close to where the power comes into your house. For many homes, that is in the basement, or if the house is on a slab, perhaps a closet near the main power lines. Look for a sizable gray metal box with lots of fat cable wires coming in and going out.

Behind a little metal door, there will be lots of breaker switches most likely in two vertical rows. There will be one long breaker switch along the top of the column.

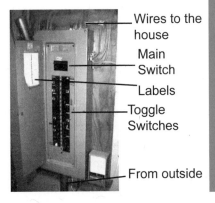

Wires to the house

Main Switch

Labels

Toggle Switches

From outside

The biggest breaker is the actual main breaker that controls power to the entire house. The rows of little breaker switches control the lines branching out to the rooms. They carry 120 volts, the norm for small appliances and fixtures. Some breakers are doubled up for the big 240-volt electric eaters: electric water heaters, dryers, ranges, ovens, and electric room heaters, if you have any.

Label your breaker switches

If the breakers aren't labeled, you have some fun work ahead of you. It helps to have another person doing this with you. Turn on everything in the house. Then one of you stands by the circuit breaker box and switches off just one breaker while the other person figures out what went out. Don't forget that receptacles and power switches are on the same lines. You may have to try using lights in receptacles to test those along the line. When you know what line is connected to what breaker—write it down in detail on the label. One line can literally go through several rooms. For example, one line can service one bedroom's switch and three receptacles, and the adjoining bathroom's two sets of switches and a receptacle or two. Remember: when something goes wrong with the electric—this is the first place you'll go to look.

Fuse Boxes

Ancient, but still around. Fuses were the standard years ago. They come in different sizes of amperes, or amps. **Do not ever, under any circumstance, screw in a different amperage from the one originally on the line.** For example, if a 12-amp fuse is installed, don't replace it with a 20-amp fuse if the line keeps blowing out. You could burn down your house. Fuses have different size bases to tell them apart.

Fuses are a bit larger than a quarter and look like the bottom end of a light bulb with a little round window on top. When they are "bad" the window looks like it has been blasted by a little fire, which it has. They, too, are contained in a large box, somewhat like the circuit breaker box and located near the entry of the main lines into the house.

Heads Up!
There should be a sheet attached to the inside of the breaker door with room to label the breakers. If they are not labeled, it is up to you to do the labeling!

Smart Move
It is a good idea to write down on a piece of paper a description of where all the lines go and what they service. Color code them if that works. I created a spreadsheet for this information.

What to Look For

There are some danger signs around the breaker/fuse box-es. If you see these—*call the electrician immediately!*

Arcing—or signs of arcing: black marks that look like streaks of black lightning. These are burn marks meaning something is definitely wrong and about to fry—if it hasn't fried already. *Call your electrician immediately!*

Warm Switches—run your finger along the circuit break-ers. They should be room temperature—not hot. *If one of them is hot—call the electrician and follow his/her advice!*

Loose Wires—if you see any loosely connected or loose wires around the box or anywhere else...*don't touch them.* They could be live and shock you. Call your electric pro and have the pro deal with it—now!

Reverse Polarity—there is a clever little gadget every homeowner should have, that tests the polarity, as well as the functioning, of the electric receptacles. It fits in your fist and requires you to plug it into the receptacle to read it. If the polarity is backwards—i.e., the hot wire is actually hooked up to the neutral pole and vice-versa, then any polarized plug (one with one prong wider than the other) forced in will send the electric backwards into the appliance and damage or destroy it.

Following the Lines

The wires running through the house are usually flat white cables. Inside the 120-volt cables are three wires, each wrapped separately and color coded. One is wrapped in black, the "hot" wire and it carries the power into the appliance. The wire wrapped in white is the return or "neutral" wire and the third is actually bare and lies between the other two. That one is the "ground" that keeps the stray power from electrocuting you and guaranteeing that the circuits will break if overloaded. In a 240-volt cable there may be another color (red or blue) wire that is also "hot." Unless you know for a certainty, by testing, that there isn't power to the lines or the wires aren't hooked up to power yet, *don't touch the wires!*

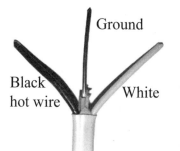

Ground

Black hot wire

White

Ground wire

The ground wire, attached to green screws in the electric boxes is there to protect you from electrocution. If a hot wire should happen to come loose and touch the metal electric box, that box and anything attached to it is "hot" and can electrocute you—as in dead. Somewhere from the circuit breaker box will be a wire heading outside again. Follow that and you will see it attached to a copper rod firmly planted in the ground. If any voltage, or electricity, gets "loose" the ground wire will direct it out of the house, shut down the circuit breaker and keep you safe. Don't mess with it! And don't try to defeat it either!

Oops!

Suppose you are using all the electronics in your office, then the kids turn on all their electronics too. And they happen to be on the same circuit line....

If your line is near or at capacity, the whole line could overload and the circuit "break" at the breaker or fuse box to prevent the house from possibly burning down.

When you go to the circuit breaker box, you'll see that one of the breakers isn't in an "on" position anymore. Before you do flip it back on, you should turn off *all* the appliances or goodies plugged into that line.

Then after you switch the breaker back on, you can restart *some* of the appliances again—one by one. Your line is overloaded. You may need to have an electrician rewire some lines to handle the bigger load on the line.

If you have a fuse box, then one of the fuses will be "blown" and look like it was hit by a mini-lightning strike. Replace it with an exactly matched fuse. If it blows again—get an electrician!

Age and code

As with plumbing, there are national, state, and probably local building codes pertaining to the wiring in your house. This is to protect you, period.

Extremely old wiring can pose a problem, as old wiring may not be up to code as the codes change and improve with available technology and supplies.

Our newer appliances and "toys" require up-to-date wiring. Your electrician can tell you if your wiring is: 1) up to code, and 2) is capable of handling modern equipment.

You can also tell by the number of holes in the receptacle. If there are three slots, the wiring is likely, but not certainly, adequate.

If there are only two slots, the wiring is not up to modern standards. If the wiring isn't up to standard or code, you could be in for a huge expense to rewire the entire house.

Also check wiring from your lamps and appliances for worn or torn spots. If you find such a spot, stop using the appliance until the wiring is replaced.

If you have to live with old wiring, *do not ever* try to defeat the grounding of adaptor plugs. You have to attach that little green wire's end to the screw in the middle of the face plate. It could conceivably save your life.

Can You Or Can You Not DIY

There are many areas in the country where DIY is not allowed when it comes to dealing with electric fixes. Sometimes it seems silly to have to call in an electrician to replace a switch that you can easily do yourself. (It only requires you to turn off the correct breaker, unscrew the face plate, pull out the switch, and one-by-one move each wire to the corresponding location on a new switch and replace everything the way it was.)

However, that is up to the local codes to determine this. You can check with the state's office dealing with construction and codes.

Before you attempt to fix anything, if you get the urge, you might check with someone in the know.

If you wish to get into this (it is actually fun stuff), buy some books on the subject! There are plenty out there. Just don't get too carried away.

There are limits on what you are allowed to do. Replacing switches and receptacles is one thing (usually legal), adding branches to the circuit breaker box is another—definitely not legal for Helga Homeowner to tackle.

Caution

ALWAYS check the amps on the switches or receptacles you plan to replace, then replace them with the same amp size, usually 15 or 20 amps.

Behind the wallplate

The inside of a switch box for two ceiling lights. Nothing mysterious here, just the 2 switches, and their wires tucked behind them. Below, a wired switch—the ground around the green screw, the white wire in the hole marked "white" and the black in the "black" hole.

Fixing It Yourself

This stuff is easy and fun. I remember having a little shelf in our rec room where I would take apart old radios and dead appliances to see how they worked. Sometimes, I could make those ancient radios work again. If you have any old busted appliances, start unscrewing the outsides and see what is inside. You may be stunned to find out how simple the whole thing is. Or more stunned to find out that the appliance really is complex.

> **Warning:** There are some appliances, those with a power supply, that have to have the power supply discharged before you touch them. Otherwise, you can get a serious electrical shock. Computers are one, if you plan to do something with the power itself, not just replacing boards. Anything with a power supply will have a warning on the supply box or the outside of the appliance. Heed the warning and leave it alone.

Get to know your hardware store electrical department. You'll find loads of different plugs, sockets, switches, and doodads for everything electrical. If you don't know what you want or need, ask a salesperson. If they don't know, find a store with someone who does!

Much of the stuff you will recognize. A switch is a switch—without a faceplate. Same with a receptacle. Wiring is pretty standard stuff. For standard electric wires to appliances and lamps, two wires run side by side, each covered with a plastic coating to keep them separate so they don't touch each other and short-out.

Exposed or broken appliance wires

Part of your tool kit should be at least one roll of electrical tape. (Chapter 9 has a tool list.) Through wear and tear, an electric cord can lose its nice protective plastic sheath exposing the wires inside. If two wires are touching, they will short out. Contact your local appliance repair

Really!
Actually, in some states it is legal to wire your own house—as long as you aren't doing it on anyone's house. It's up to you to find that out.

ACMT*
When I visited my beloved aunt, she would gather all the busted lamps to be fixed, lining them up on her dining room table for repairs.
*Auntie's Crisis Management Team

to *replace* the cord itself. Most likely, you will not find a replacement cord in the hardware store. However, here's a quick repair:

With the cord unplugged, separate the exposed wires, even if you have to slice some of the plastic sheath between the 2 wires to make room. If both wires are exposed, each needs to be wrapped with electrical tape separately, then the entire section of cord wrapped. If only one wire is exposed, wrap the entire exposed section of cord.

Lamp sockets

If you have a lamp that doesn't work and a new bulb isn't the answer, you can fix it yourself with a screwdriver, cutting pliers, and patience.

If the problem isn't the wires, perhaps the switch is shot. You may need a new socket for the bulb, which can be purchased at any hardware store. These are cheap.

To change a lamp socket

First look at the socket you are replacing, then buy an identical socket.

Unplug the lamp and remove the lampshade and bulb.

Look at the metal socket cover. Somewhere along the crimped part will be a notation to Press Here. Do so with your thumb, push up to remove the sheath out of the base to expose the wires.

Unscrew the little flat screws to remove the wires and pull the old socket off the wires and lamp. Slide the new socket into place. Screw the wires to the same screws on the new socket, replace the sheath and snap it into place.

Now replace the bulb, plug it in and test it.

Rewiring a lamp

You can use the same opening scenario to replace non-polarized plugs and wires in a lamp. Wire can be purchased by the foot at hardware stores. Don't forget to purchase a plug—the kind that snaps onto the end of the wire.

Safey Tip

Any bare electric wires touching each other can cause a short and potentially a fire. Not to mention electrocuting someone.

If you notice any wires like this—or any hot wires on an appliance cord, have them checked professionally.

Tools: screwdriver, utility or pocket knife, and needlenose pliers with cutters are best for this.

Unplug the lamp, remove the bulb, remove the metal sheath and its insulation, unscrew the wires and pull them through the bottom of the lamp.

Feed your new wire up into the lamp where the old wire came out.

Push the wire about 4–5" out of the top so it is easy to play with.

Slit down the cord in the middle about 2–3" between the two wires without cutting into or removing any of the plastic around the wires. There is a noticeable guide to do this. A sharp pocket knife works quite well for this.

Remove the top inch of plastic off each wire. This is accomplished by carefully "cutting" down into the plastic with a knife blade or proper cutter and twisting the cutter around slowly until you hit the wire, then pull off the plastic.

Using your fingers, twist each wire so none of the little strands separate.

With the pliers, bend the entire wire to fit around the appropriate screw. Usually, it doesn't matter which wire goes around which screw, but sometimes they are color-coded with the gold referring to the black or hot wire and the silver representing the white or neutral wire. If you put the wire on the left side of the screw and wrap it to the right, then when you twist the screw down, the wires will stay where you want them instead of blasting out from behind the screw. Try to make sure the strands stay together. Stray ones can break the contact so the lamp doesn't work.

When the wires are in place, gently pull the extra wire from the bottom until the socket just about sits where it belongs. You do want a bit of slack.

Replace the metal sheath and insulation and snap them into place.

Safety Tip

Hot wires could mean a break and short inside the wire.

Snap the plug onto the other end of the wire. Screw i
the bulb and test the lamp.

Fluorescent Ballast

**Fluore-
scent
Ballasts**

Some
smaller
fluorescent
lamps have
small "tube"
ballasts
about 2"
long that
are easily
removed
by pushing
in and
twisting
out of their
position.

If your large fixture's fluorescent bulbs are working ju
fine, but sputtering, it could be the ballast needs to l
replaced.

If you remove the cover of the fixture, you will see a hea
black box, usually sitting between two tubes. It is a fai
costly item, around $20 or so, and found in hardwa
stores. There will be a number on the ballast giving y
the type and style. Buy the identical replacement.

After the cover of the fixture is removed, the circ
breaker turned off, the switch to the fixture turned o
you can unscrew the little caps to the wires connecti
the ballast to the lamp.

Carefully unscrew and remove the ballast. Now repl
the new ballast where the old one was and screw i
place, twist the white wires to the white wires, the bl
to the black on both ends, replace the caps, replace
fixture cover and turn everything on again.

Chapter 9

Preparing for Repairs

Inevitably, appliances, roofs, light bulbs, switches, and a variety of things will need replacing. Stands to reason, you finally get to understand everything, know where it is and what it does, and whammo! It breaks. If you prepare yourself ahead of time for the little/big future nasties, they won't be as much of a surprise.

Everything related to a house has a life expectancy. At some point, it will fail. If you keep on top of the maintenance, or at least keep an eye on everything and notice when something isn't right, you can go a long way towards making sure that the life expectancy is a long one.

Finding the right repair professional

If at all possible, establish a working relationship with repair pros well ahead of any emergency. Especially those involved with your plumbing, electrical, and heating/cooling systems. Add to that list a qualified appliance repair person. Get references from friends whose judgement you trust, and who have used the pro in question. If they don't have any ideas, check with contractors who work with these people. If you don't get any help there, start calling the Yellow Pages entries. The biggest ad isn't always the best company to deal with. Scope out the company. Do you like what they say? Do they put you off? (Bad sign.) A refrigerator or freezer needing repairs is an emergency to good repair people. These repairs are first on the list. This is a judgement call on your part if you are calling blind.

Replacing Appliances

Schedule
Just as you maintain your vehicle with oil changes and lubes, you should do this with your house.

There comes a time in every appliance's life when it should be recycled in the steel bin at the dump. You may really love that old dishwasher, but when it costs more to fix it or to run it than to replace it, then loosen your wallet and replace it.

When to fix it yourself

If you are a handy sort and love tinkering with appliances, do so! At least give it a try. Many times, you can find the simple answer and fix it yourself. There are many books with exact instructions on how to repair all sorts of appliances. You can find these books in hardware stores, book stores, and the like. Reader's Digest has a wonderful book, *Householder's Survival Manual*, loaded with all sorts of how-tos and what-tos.

Oops!
If the breakdown occurs during the weekend and the job can wait, by all means, wait to call until a weekday.

You'll save yourself the overtime and extra charges for a weekend repair.

Many appliance manufacturers have websites with pages on fixes you can manage, or help you decide if the appliance needs a major repair. To get to the site, type in the manufacturer's name in the URL. For example: typing "ge" will get you www.ge.com, or a list of searched sites with "ge" in them. Click on Appliances, then the Answer Center. Many times, the fix is so simple you really can do it yourself and save the money and wasted time. At least you can find out whether you have something to call a pro about. It will narrow down the choices, giving the pro a better understanding of your problem.

When to call for help

If you can't handle minor repairs and prefer calling a repair pro, by all means, do so! Your life is worth something, too. Assuming you have found the repair pro of your dreams, make the call.

If the job is an emergency repair (i.e., refrigerator or freezer), call the office and explain the problem.

Before you call

First of all, you need to know what the appliance is: make, model, year; and what is wrong with the appliance. This may sound dumb—yeah, yeah, if I knew, I could fix it! Duh. Well, no. You should be able to pinpoint a problem and tell the repair service at least what is the effect of the problem. Say it's a washer that isn't draining correctly—you can articulate that. (But first, check the drain pipes at the back to make sure they aren't kinked or bent.) Suppose the dishwasher makes some rather strange noises and doesn't clean—describe the noises and if you listen carefully while it is running, if it is able to work, you might be able to tell where the noise comes from—i.e., the top of the machine, back, bottom? It is a dull thud? Or a sharp noise? You get the idea.

From this information, perhaps the repair service can give you an idea what is wrong and how much it usually costs to fix. If the machine is old, it may be better to replace it.

Life expectancy

All appliances have a "life expectancy" of so many years. If the fix is costly, consider replacement. However, as the base prices of appliances have remained the same, but the cost of manufacturing an appliance hasn't, the parts are now made of lesser quality materials, while the "goodie" factor has increased. The "goodie" factor is the improvements made to the overall operation or appearance of the appliance: easier to clean, faster operation, saves more energy, and so forth.

If your appliance is 10+ years old, and it is repairable, you might consider keeping it. The lower-priced "modern" appliances are designed to survive 3–4 years without repairs. The high-end appliances, the costly ones, are designed to last longer without repairs. Would you rather keep an old trustworthy functioning "pal" that may need an occasional repair? Or will you put up with a shiny new appliance that may need repairs frequently. However, consider the energy efficiency or cost of running the appliance.

Remember

Pros have a life, too, and hope to have their weekends to themselves and their own families.

But an emergency is something taken seriously.

They will respond.

Life expectancies of appliances in years

Below is a list of major appliances and how long they are expected to live, as well as how much you can expect to pay to replace them—at least as a starting point:

	Years	Low	Mid	High
Range	15–20	$400	$600	$2000
Clothes Washer	5–10	$350	$500	$2000
Clothes Dryer	7–11	$300	$400	$500
Dishwasher	7–12	$300	$400	$650
Refrigerator	8–15	$550	$700	$3000

Efficiency
Check the energy efficiency numbers on the yellow labels on any new appliance you are looking to buy.

Compare the cost of the replacement, its eventual repair costs (ask about how much it is to repair a major component), and the stress factor of having to spend the time away from work being there for the delivery crew's eventual arrival, the disposal costs and how to dispose of the dead appliance versus a repair on your current appliance.

An honest repair pro can help you with this decision. Ask the pro's opinion. If the parts are hard to get, it may be time for a replacement.

Every year, appliances are more and more energy efficient, or supposed to be—something to keep in mind when considering your options. Check with your local power company as many will offer rebates on energy efficient models, or at least point you in the direction of the most efficient units.

Instead of putting a wad of money into repairing an old appliance that costs a lot to run, it could be far more cost effective for you to replace the appliance with a newer, energy efficient one that saves you its purchase price in energy over the next few years.

Check out *Consumer Reports* magazine—if you don't subscribe, look for it in your library—for their ratings, or ask your repair pro (hopefully an unbiased one) for an opinion, and check out various internet sites for comparisons.

When our dishwasher bit the garbage once too often, I started washing the dishes every night—to the tune of three hours spent washing the dishes and kitchen instead of working. After three weeks of this, my spouse broke down and told me to get one *now!* It wasn't worth my time wasted in the kitchen. Your time is worth something too. Don't forget that when dealing with recalcitrant appliances.

Sometimes the repair is simplicity itself and worth doing. Ask your trusted repair service what their judgement is and evaluate it yourself. Don't get pushed into replacing a perfectly fine appliance that can be fixed easily and cheaply.

Before you decide that your appliance is dead, check the cord—is the appliance really plugged in? Next step, check any fuses in the appliance (some do have them) or at the circuit breaker to the appliance, or pull out the appliance's plug and try plugging in a lamp or small appliance you can tell works (i.e., a hairdryer). If the lamp works, the appliance is receiving electricity. If the appliance has water pipes, check those—any kinks, obvious holes in the lines, disconnected? If all the "Gee, I should have tried *that!*" things don't work, time to call in help.

Costs
While a very efficient one may cost more to purchase—over the life of the appliance, it will cost you less.

One of my friends called me, almost hysterical, that her computer monitor wasn't working, she had a 5:00 PM deadline and needed to print out her manuscript. From her description, I told her to check the cord to the monitor, it sounded as if it had loosened itself. She didn't believe me. But I insisted. When she finally did look, sure enough… the cord was just about hanging out of the socket.

If you bought this appliance recently, and it's giving you grief…what is the warranty or do you have one? Did you get an extended warranty? Is it still good? Asking for help nicely reaps rewards, tenfold.

When one of the screws on our not-yet-one-year-old washer broke and completely trashed the clothes basket assembly, I called the place where I purchased it and explained the situation to the owner/manager in a calm and downright friendly manner. He offered an equitable trade. I return the machine for a full credit (it was a dented one anyway, purchased for $300) and he would give me that credit towards any other I chose. We got another dented gem for $330—minus the $300 credit, it cost me another $30. Big deal. Afterwards, I wrote him a thank you letter that went a long way towards sealing a friendship and helping the next person in trouble.

Just Making Sure!
Always check the warranty on any appliance you purchase. The longer the original warranty, usually, the better the product, as the manufacturer doesn't expect it to come back to haunt them.

Replace cheap or otherwise

If you have plenty of cash to spend, by all means get what you want the first time. If you don't have money to throw around, here are some ways to save and still get what you want.

Dented and bashed

Every appliance store has the corner where they stash the dented goods, or perhaps returned but still warrantied and/or refurbished goods. If you are careful and wise, you can get a top quality appliance for up to half the retail price. Just ask the salespeople about them. They will point you in the right direction. Besides, who will know you have a dented fridge if the dents don't show in your kitchen? Just check to make sure the dents aren't damaging the interior of the appliance or its operation. Those are usually sent back to the manufacturer directly anyway—but checking is a good idea.

Buy used

Some appliance stores also have used appliances for sale. These were taken in trade, or purchased cheaply and refurbished for resale. Make sure anything you buy this way has a warranty or, if possible, some sort of service deal. If it is "as is" it had better be cheap, because you are gambling!

Years ago, my sister, a caterer, bought our old dying fridge (real cheap) for one last job to cool the canapes at a party she was catering. As luck would have it, the fridge worked fine, until the party ended. It sighed and died.

How to choose?

One way to decide what you need with a brand, spanking new appliance is start with your dream appliance: what do you want it to have? List it all. Price that appliance. If it isn't affordable for you now in perfect condition, look in the dented section. Not available, then one by one, scratch out the things you really don't need as you go down the price list into the price category you can afford. For example: you need a new clothes washer and just love all the fancy choices of timings, cycles and load sizes.

If you are a practical sort, start with the energy efficient washers—the front loaders. If you have a family, do you need a large capacity washer? Or will a normal capacity washer do? Do you wash seriously filthy clothing, or finer cleaner fabrics? Do you really need all the washing choices offered? If not, look for a more basic machine that does the job you need done.

For all the goodies packed into the higher priced appliances, how many of those extras are you really, really going to use? If you wash the same stuff all the time, do you need a washer with 10 fancy options? Or maybe one or two other options? When cooking, if you are a fancy chef, you may need or want a bunch more options than a cook like me—heat it and serve! (Okay, I'm not *that* bad!)

Be Energy Wise

Choose appliances for their low **Energy Rating** or see if any are **Energy Star** rated by the U.S. Government. You will save a substantial amount of money over the lifetime of the appliance.

Preparing for Big Ticket Items

All these systems have a life expectancy of so many years. Therefore, you should have an idea of how long you plan to remain in the house, and if you are really clever, you found out when you bought the house, just how old all these following systems are.

Heads UP

When buying asphalt roofing, checking the warranty on the package can give you a good idea of the expected lifespan of your shingles once installed. Some shingles are only warrantied for 10 years, others up to 25 years or more.

If you are good at budgeting, you might consider putting some money aside every month for future use—because without fail, something will fail. Keep an eye on these systems by checking them, at least yearly (see the section on Yearly Checkups), and head off trouble before it gets outrageously expensive. That old "penny saved" adage is priceless. If you do take proper care of your house, you shouldn't have these problems.

Roofs

This system is critical. Without a good roof, your house is worthless. If you have an asphalt single roof, the shingles can last 10–25 years depending on the quality of the shingles themselves. "Replacing a roof" can be as simple as covering the roof with another layer of shingles (buy only the top quality and save yourself lots of grief later), or rebuilding the entire roof—a very expensive proposition. Clarifying the term "replacing the roof" is essential.

Here is a list of the types of roofing and their expected lifespan. Hopefully, when you bought your house, you found out when the roof was last replaced (from the former owners or from your inspection report).

Roof Life Expectancies in years:

Asphalt Shingle	15–30
Slate Tiles	50–200
Clay Tile	50–100
Wood Shakes	15+
Wood Shingle	10+
Metal	35+

When the time comes to work on your roof, hire only the best established, roofing contractor with plenty of excellent references. It is, by far, the least expensive way to do it. The cost may seem high initially, but the best crews are worth their weight in platinum. Even if the job is just to reshingle the roof, hire the best.

> Recently a friend had her roof fixed. She had, in fact, hired the best. As she was explaining the job to me she, at first, thought the fee quite high— until she realized that the contractor had upwards of 10 men on her roof for two full days. The job was done correctly, on time, and on schedule with little disruption to her life. That alone saved her money as she is also a freelance writer. In retrospect, she thought she did quite well.

Septic Systems (rural situations)

If you have a septic system, you should know by now what comprises the system and, hopefully, where it is located from "Getting to Know Your House" when you moved in.

Generally well-built systems can last forever if pumped properly and maintained on a reasonable schedule. If the system fails, it is an expensive propositon and only the pros can build you another—to code.

If the situation arises that is outside of the house, you need to check with the septic tank contractor or "honey wagon" companies. The "honey wagon" is a euphemism for the big tank full of pumped septic tank contents. In the "old days" the liquid collection was generally first "cleaned" with lime, then taken to a willing farmer's field to be spread as fertilizer. Think about this next time you wish to flush something you don't want seen again.

Nowadays, the honeywagon contents are taken to a proper sewage treatment facility and dealt with there. Which is why the cost to clean septic tanks has gone up.

Heads UP
A rural rule of thumb is: If you didn't eat it or drink it first, it doesn't go down the toilet.

Heating/Cooling Systems

Some heating (and heating/cooling) systems just putter along forever without a care. Don't you wish. All heating/cooling systems require yearly maintenance of some sort and are designed to last at least 15–20 years. If yours is approaching its dotage, have the system assessed as to whether or not it will survive another decade or so, or how much longer can it cope.

Another Mantra
Do it Right the First Time!

If your system fails miserably, and can't be fixed, consider replacing it with a much more energy-efficient model. It should pay for itself quickly in energy not used and wasted.

Here is a chart of the lifespan of heating systems:

Oil, Gas and Electric furnaces	15–25 years
Steel boilers	15–25 years
Cast Iron boilers	20–40 years
Heat pump compressors	8–12 years

Replacing your system is a matter of what is practical. Do you replace it with a similar system, but the updated version? Or is something else more practical? If you have a water-based system, replacing it with a forced air system would be foolish as you would have to replace all the piping throughout the house.

If you are a woodstove-based household, adding an appropriately sized propane heater is an easy choice. Whatever your choice, make sure you get the correct size unit for your house. Heating systems are rated by how many BTU (British Thermal Units) it requires to heat how much space. You need to know or have the HVAC pro figure out exactly how many cubic feet "big" your house is. Then you look for the appropriately sized equipment. Don't think you'll save money by buying a smaller unit. All you'll do, besides freezing to death, is waste money feeding the thing and still not get warm enough.

Of course, that goes for buying too big a unit. Overkill in the heating department can be a big waste of money too.

One contractor conned a hapless homeowner into three different heating systems via Change Orders. As the second unit was being installed, he called another contractor for advice and was told he only needed one system and to make sure the others were removed from the house—and from his final bill. They were.

Dealing with the little repairs

Never entered a hardware store, home improvement mega store, or a lumber yard before? Personally, I prefer the hardware store to clothing stores. Sorry, but I always have.

I love tinkering with new tools and fixing stuff. I learned by taking things apart, then putting them back together again. Most of the time they still worked just fine, thank you. (The watch didn't—I couldn't find the pieces after the mainspring shot all over the rec room.)

This book isn't going to tell you how to fix problems, that's another bunch of books altogether—and there are plenty of them out there if you are so inclined. There are so many little niggly repairs and fixes you can do yourself without instruction that we offer these basic tools to have on hand—just in case.

Many of the megahome improvement stores hold classes for homeowners who are interested in learning how to install, build, or otherwise use tools. If you like the idea—sign up for classes! They are held on weekends and occasionally evenings. The classes are free. Bring your curiosity and don't wear anything you don't want ruined!

You might wish to get a copy of *About the House with Henri de Marne* (Upper Access Publishing, ISBN 978-0-942679-30-4), but he has been writing his syndicated column, *First Aid for the Ailing House* for over 30 years now dealing with questions from readers asking about problems with their home and what to do to correct the problem.

Minimal Set of Tools

Some things you can't do without. You can buy this set of stuff as a small toolkit or separately. Depending on how fancy your choices are, the basics can be purchased for less than $50 (real basic) up to $100. There is that little kit I bought for my mother for a whopping $15 in a mass-market department store. You might look for one if you aren't really a tool person. Visit the local hardware store or chain department stores to start your collection.

Get a toolbox to store these in, so they are all in the same place at the same time. If there are small children around, make sure you store these where they can't get at them.

Tools and items to have on hand

The Basics:

√ Screwdrivers: Phillips head (the one with the × tip)—at least small and medium-size flathead screwdrivers, these can be bought in sets inexpensively. There are great ratcheting screwdriver sets where one shaft takes several tips in various sizes and shapes. Sometimes, these are just as expensive as buying a collection set of screwdrivers. Ratchet sets are easier to use.

√ Pliers, standard or even better—Channellock® is one brand that's quite good, or Vise-Grip® locking pliers. They are different in the way they grip.

√ Needlenose pliers (the pointy ones)

√ Screws, nuts and bolts, brads, and small nails

√ Duct tape

√ Measuring tape—8 feet should be fine, but for bigger stuff, use a 25-foot by 1"

√ Hammer—one that is comfortable for you to heft without breaking your wrist (if you have to hold it higher up on the shaft, aka "choking," that's cool too)

√ Utility knife

√ Heavy duty stapler (not your office variety)

√ Hacksaw or little handsaw

√ Adjustable wrench

Leatherman!

Not the nightshow guy—the tool! All of these can be bought as one cool folding unit called a Leatherman or some similar tool collection. The tiny version, called a Micra, is a wonder to keep handy in your purse or pocket.

You can buy an inexpensive tool box that should be quite adequate for around the house futzing, for about $20 or so at your local hardware store. That's what I gave my mother years ago. She wouldn't be without it.

Getting more into this:

√ Electrical tape

√ Socket wrench set

√ Wonder Bar® (removes nails and pry things apart)

√ Little level (handy for hanging pictures), or even bigger 2-foot level

√ Square of some sort—"tri square" or the bigger "framing square"—these are used to make corners square

√ Cutter pliers—for cutting wires, or look for pliers with the cutter built in

Electrical specific extras

√ Voltage tester

√ Stripper

√ (still have electrical tape?)

√ A collection of "caps" ⟶

Plumbing specific extras

√ Adjustable wrenches—bigger one for heavy-duty plumbing jobs

√ Collection of rubber washers

√ Plunger for the toilet

√ Gordon Wrench

Wood-related extras (power tools)—if you really get into this!

√ Drill (1/4" will do fine for starters) and bits. You can buy these in a small collection covering plenty of sizes. One bit does not fit all.

√ Handsaw—a better, more professional one

√ Power saw

√ Whatever else grabs your practical fancy

Big Hint

Before you start busting your wrist twisting a screw in place, try "greasing" it up with a bit of old bar soap. It will go in much more easily.

Yard tools

√ Lawn mower—if you don't hire someone else to do the job

√ Leaf rake

√ Shovel—there are various types so figure out what you want to use the shovel for, then get the appropriate one

√ Snow shovel (for snow country)

√ Garden trowels and assorted pronged things

When my Master Gardener friend, Maggie Nocca read this last line about "assorted pronged things" she laughed herself silly, then decided it was time *The Savvy Woman's Guide to Gardening* was finally written. Obviously, her friend, Kitty, was not a gardener of note, otherwise the list would have some serious gardening tools on it.

Chapter 10

Seasonal To-Do List

This chapter will help you follow some sort of schedule for checking around your house and keeping things functioning and in good repair.

Some of this simply won't apply to you. If you live where it doesn't snow, don't worry about the cold weather stuff, and vice versa. If you don't have a fireplace or woodstove, you don't need firewood or to have your chimney cleaned. If your heating season is only one month long—maybe this isn't critical.

If your heating season is six months long, then this is more than critical, it could save your life if the power goes out for any length of time.

Summer

Order firewood—snow country

This may seem seriously silly to order firewood this early, unless you live up north where prices fluctuate according to seasons and availability. For you northerners, especially if your area is prone to power outages, make sure you always have some on hand. The earlier you order it, the cheaper it is.

Firewood as it is cut is often "green," meaning that it still has moisture from growing (unless the tree was pretty well dead before cutting in which case it could be punky, therefore useless).

"Seasoned" wood is dry, or has been dried out. Green wood is hard to burn and smokes, without giving out a lot of heat. Seasoned wood burns hot, but more quickly, but is the ideal. If you buy wood well before you need it, you can dry out the wood yourself and save money on the difference between green and seasoned wood. Stack it in the open so that air can get through it.

Quick Dry Wood
If you are pushed for time, stack the wood in a sunny spot and cover the pile with plastic. Cut holes in the plastic around the top of the pile to allow the moisture to evaporate.

Check the outside structures for repairs

If you have outside decks, stairs and other "out buildings," check them for splinters, cracks, popping nails, or any other signs of aging or falling apart. A quick repair now could spare you big bucks later on. Periodically, give them a thorough once-over, checking underneath, around and inside, just everywhere. If it isn't a repair you can handle, find someone who can do it properly. (See the chapter on hiring contractors.)

Arrange the seasonal (snow-country)

For you snowbelt dwellers, now is the time to make sure you have arranged any snowplowing necessary. Don't wait until the first dump to think about this, you could be stuck at home for a long time. Look for a competent plower, one who will consider your requirements when the time comes. Signing up with someone who won't plow you during a crisis until after dinner doesn't help if you need to be out to work at 8:00 AM.

Fall

Insulation

Remember last winter (or summer) and the spots of too hot or too cold? Maybe the insulation isn't what it should be. Some types of insulation can compact or get eaten by mice, or be slept in by unwanted visitors, becoming less useful. If you know what type of insulation you have, and you know you have a problem, find a contractor (or your builder) and have someone look at it now. Make note of where the problem is to save valuable time.

Check windows and doors

Check seals and gaskets around the windows and doors and replace them as necessary. This is an easy job, but if you can't do it, find someone who can. It can mean the difference between a cold drafty winter and high heat bills or a warm, comfy winter. (See Chapter 12.)

Faucets—outside (snow states)

Drain outside faucets and turn off the water to them. There will be a valve inside the house where you have to shut off the water supply, then go outside and open the faucet to allow any water still inside to drain out before it freezes. Some "stop and drain" valves have a little knurl on the bottom to allow you to empty any remaining water.

If you have frost-proof faucets (it is indicated somewhere on the front plate as well as the design—the faucet will stick straight out instead of have an angle up—to allow the water to drain), you don't have to worry about this.

Clean chimneys and woodstoves

You do not want a chimney fire of any sort. A bad one can explode, sending burning chunks flying around the neighborhood, not to mention burning your house down. The best prevention is cleaning your chimney, fireplace and/or woodstoves—*before* you use them.

Look for an experienced, qualified chimney sweep. Good sweeps can and should be certified. When you call, you need to tell the sweep how many flues you have, and if you know, what material they are made of: stainless steel, clay tile, or maybe—in many old historic houses—there isn't any liner at all. That is a crisis waiting to happen.

If you don't have any liner, the quickest way to line a flue is with stainless steel and insulation. It is a very safe liner and fairly easy to install when done properly. In Peter's experience, poured liners can expand and crack the chimney—especially if you have a chimney fire.

Don't Forget
Drain and put away all outside hoses.

Safety Tip
Over the summer, birds or other critters can make nests in your chimney which will give you quite a fireworks show if you start a fire and the nest catches. Either that, or you might find your house filled with noxious smoke.

Handy for the heating season:

√ bottle of ACS—Anti-Creo-Soot, a product used to spray wood when cold, that cleans out the worst (Class 3) creosote from a chimney and essentially cleans it up

√ chimney fire extinguisher—made by Chimflex, it is about one foot long by one inch thick that you snap and heave into the fire—it puts the fire out—or at least helps contain it

√ regular fire extinguisher nearby, but *away* from the fireplace or stove and easy to reach

Heating systems checked and cleaned

If you have a system that requires burning (i.e., fuel-fired), call your heating supply company and have them inspect and clean your system. Hopefully, these are the people you checked out when you first moved in (see Chapter 2—Get Functional).

If it is a water system, you might have the whole system checked for air. This can prevent some areas or rooms from heating properly.

If you have electric heat, the registers get dusty with disuse and stink as the dust burns off the first time you use the heat. Vacuum out the baseboard units.

Check fuel supplies

If you have tanks for your fuel supply, make sure the tanks are filled before the first cold snap or snowfall. If you are short of cash, ask about the budget plan.

See if you are on a delivery schedule. If you have huge tanks, maybe you aren't on a schedule and need to call to schedule a delivery.

Cover the shrubs

If you live in cold climates and have bushes or flowers that need protecting, do so before the first frost. Bushes near houses need protection from snow sliding down off

Heads UP
Keep drapes and burnables away from any registers and heat sources.

Warning
One family was burned out of their house because a mouse nest built inside the electric register wasn't cleaned out before they turned the heat on!

These are mini-maples growing in a gutter!

the roof. A sandwich board type frame put over the bush is one way to solve the problem.

Roses need some sort of insulating protection.

Clean the gutters

Falling leaves or pine needles tend to clog gutters, so the gutters can't drain properly. If you don't have trees dropping offerings, then this probably isn't a problem. Just keep your eye on the gutters for other damage anyway.

Order firewood—if not already done

Check your supply, is it enough? Is it dry? If not, you might consider getting some drier wood and/or kindling.

If you live around pine trees, collect the cones for fire starter material. They are wonderful. During a "mast" year (when there is a major fall of cones) fill as many bags as you can to store the cones. They last a long time.

Winter

Clean or at least have chimney checked

Yet again, if you are using the fireplace or stove, have that chimney swept or at least checked. Don't take chances, this is cheap "insurance." If you have doubts about this, at least get some advice about your own situation from your sweep and follow that.

Check smoke, CO detectors

Test those detectors every month. Replace the batteries at least once a year, even if you tested them and they were "ok" then. You don't want to take chances with your life or those of your family.

Ice Dams! Ice dams are caused by inadequate ventilation of your roof. The roof should have ventilation through soffits so air can circulate under the roof itself allowing the roof to remain cold.

This is a serious ice dam problem. No insulation or ventilation in the roof.

Check roof for leaks, ice dams

Watch for ice build-up at the ends of your roof. If you have icicles hanging from your roof, you may have a problem to fix later. When the roof is dried up, check the roof for broken shingles or other damage. Take a look in the attic for leaks caused by ice build up. If your roof doesn't have proper ventilation, you may need to have that situation corrected over the summer. Otherwise, you could be facing a major roof repair bill. Get the best contractor to do it. See Chapter 23—Finding a Contractor for more information.

Spring

Undo winterizing

√ Uncover the plants,

√ Open the outdoor faucets

√ Check the slope around the foundation for proper drainage—away from the house

√ Check air-conditioning—filters need to be changed?

√ Have chimney cleaned

√ Check roof for leaks—get any repaired

Chapter 11

Yearly Check-up

Much of what follows, if needing repair, must be done by a well-established contractor. If and when you need the services of a contractor—read Chapter 23–Finding a Contractor *first*.

It doesn't hurt to be curious about what is happening with your house. Most of these nasties won't happen to you. But if they do, don't panic first. Save it for later—if the news is really bad. If you don't want to hassle with trying to figure out what's going on, call on that expert. Remember our mantra: "Nothing is obvious to the uninformed!" You didn't build the house, you own it. Big difference. You are probably an expert in an entirely different field.

Once a year, preferably when it is sunny and warm, so you can see everything, walk around your house, with a flashlight for the dark spots and take a look at the places that you don't normally inspect or see all the time and make note of any changes. You don't have to be an inspector yourself to do this. You will notice cracks in the walls, nails you trip over and so forth.

Understand that houses "settle" down over the years, and move seasonally due to humidity or lack of it. Soils shift, water tables rise and fall depending on rainfalls and droughts. All this affects your home. When you first move in make note of what condition the house is in—make a note of anything unusual (to you) then watch in the future for any changes.

No slights
When we say, "If you can't do it yourself," we are presuming you are either too busy, or simply don't have the inclination to do it. This is not meant as a slight. We're being practical about the situation.

Yearly Check-up

Basements and Foundations

The important point here is keeping the house on a stable, whole foundation. If you notice cracks in upstairs walls, don't wait for your "yearly" inspection. Go look now. And start at the bottom! You need to look on the inside walls—and the outside walls, as well as all the nooks and crannies. If you are squeamish about touching potentially gooky stuff, wear plastic gloves. You may have to move plants around, or pull off cobwebs to get to some of these places. Don't hesitate to do it. Take a good look at your structure.

Urgency!
If the crack is sudden, call a competent contractor immediately. Watch for water coming in these cracks.

Cracks and leaks

Hairline cracks usually aren't serious. They happen all the time. Keep an eye on them as they could be leading to something far more serious. To check on these cracks, take paper with you and using a pencil make a "rubbing" of the crack, and mark the spot where you made the rubbing. Go back in a week or month and compare the rubbing against the crack. If it is bigger, this calls for action. If it is exactly the same, don't worry about it.

If the crack is greater than hairline on an inside wall, it could result from a structural fault, or perhaps insufficient reinforcement used in the wall itself. You can tell if the cracks are moving by smearing a strip of plaster of paris (obtained from the hardware store) over part of the crack. If the cracks reappear, something more is going on. This situation needs to be dealt with by a pro. If the cracks aren't growing or shifting, and no water is leaking in, keep an eye on it.

This is a structural crack in a concrete foundation looking at it from the outside of the house.

Where is the leak coming from? If you are looking at it from the inside of the house and there is nothing obvious, go outside to determine where the problem is coming from. The ground should slope down and away from the house which will lead water away from the basement. If the slope is allowing water to cruise down along your basement wall, change the slope first. (Yeah, I know the plants want the water! Deal with it another way, as in water them separately and just enough—don't drown them and therefore your basement walls.) There is a caveat here: you don't want to build up your ground over the waterproofing (usually black gook smeared on the wall, coming up from underground; technical name: bitumen waterproofing) around the basement foundation.

If that doesn't do the trick... there is another reason for the seepage. Is your foundation really waterproofed? If not, then the ground has to be removed, the drainage checked, or installed correctly, the walls waterproofed, dried and the ground replaced.

Do not waterproof block walls from the inside. Water can get trapped inside the hollow parts of the block and rot out parts of your house. Instead you may need an inside drainage system installed. This is done by a pro.

Supposing the wall is cracked bigtime—this isn't just a leak, your foundation is possibly collapsing (see the next paragraph on Collapsing Walls), or perhaps the house has settled down unevenly. While settling is normal, if the cracks are big, they do need professional attention and quickly. Those cracks must be filled and secured. There are many ways of dealing with this: from epoxy injections, coatings, parging (smearing a concrete-like stuff over the wall), to replacing the walls entirely. This is "call in the expert" time. A worst case scenario is having to rebuild the walls, or dig out the foundation and repair it, or a not-so-drastic method is to repair the wall from the inside.

Collapsing walls

Check your basement walls, even in the dark and yucky corners, for any cracks. Use a good light to really *see* the wall. Get to know the cracks—where they are and how big, even if you have to draw little diagrams for yourself to remember them from year to year.

If the cracks are greater than 1/8", *especially if they are sudden, your foundation could be at risk of collapsing!* Take a

Membrane? Check for a waterproof membrane around your foundation. If there is one, are there tears in it? If so, they must be repaired.

More serious cracking—to be dealt with asap!

walk around the house, checking the outside for pressure points. If you had a lot of rain recently, maybe the ground swelled and pushed in the walls. This can happen when the foundation walls made of eight-inch block are buried in the ground more than 5–6 feet. This is a common practice, but that doesn't mean it is a good practice. Whether or not it is a serious potential problem depends on your soils, drainage and a number of other factors.

Horizontal cracks in block walls, especially in the middle of the wall, are signs that your walls are caving in, or the blocks are shifting. This usually happens 2 to 4 courses of block below grade (dirt level). Essentially, this means the wall is under severe pressure. If this is true, you need immediate help to fix this—call your contractor and have them assess the situation.

There are several ways to deal with this situation. Here are two:

√ build a steel- and concrete-reinforced wall with at least one right angle in front of the damaged wall;

√ rebuild the foundation itself including digging out the damaged area from the outside and rebuilding the wall itself with poured concrete (probably most expensive, but best solution);

Obviously, these require a contractor and expertise. Use the best, not the cheapest, contractor.

Crawl spaces

Important place this, if you have one. Houses are either built on a slab with nothing underneath that bottom floor but cement; or over a crawl space—named because that's the only way to get around down there; or a basement which may or may not be used by the homeowner for anything other than storage.

There are two sides to the following issue: moisture and ventilation of crawls paces. Some experts and the old codes tell you, that you have to have the area ventilated; others tell you that's insane. Lately, the National Association of

Heads UP

If water is gushing in, you really have a problem —*call in the experts now!*

Warning

If a pro suggests a buttress in this situation, find another pro. Bad idea, buttresses don't work.

Home Builders (NAHB) has done new research saying that ventilation is a bad idea and is changing the code.

It all depends on where you live, the type of climate, soil conditions, where exactly the house is located, construction and plenty of other variables.

Crawl spaces need to be checked for water, moisture, cracked walls, rotting wood, rotted posts, evidence of pests and anything else unusual. There should be a layer of thick plastic sheeting (at least 6-mil) over the entire dirt floor. It should be overlapped (at least a foot or more, and/or taped into one piece) in such a way that no moisture can get through to your house to rot out the underneath of your floors overhead.

If there is plastic down there and it is disturbed, torn or otherwise not doing its job, replace it immediately. And find out why it failed.

If you have a stacked stone foundation (old farmhouses are notorious for this) it could be that little wild animals have invaded your crawl space and made it a home. If so, you may want to seal up the openings in the stones. The most effective way is with mortar. Either buy a bag of Sakcrete® Mortar Mix, read the instructions to mix it properly and trowel it in yourself; or even better—call an expert (see Chapter 22 on Finding a Contractor). Trusted expert opinions are extremely valuable. Treat them as such. They could save your house and investment many times over.

Above is a bulging stone and brick foundation being pushed inward by outside water pressure.

Chimneys and fireplaces

Chimneys are not always attached to a house: some are an integral part of the house, others stand beside the house. Outside chimneys settle down on their own if their foundation is separate from the house foundation. Some cracks are normal, others, plainly, are not. If you notice tiny cracks between the bricks and the mortar, it's a fair chance that the mortar wasn't the correct mix or the mortar didn't have a chance to cure properly. It's quite common—but not a cause for alarm.

The cracks follow the line of the mortar that didn't "stick."

Make sure the chimney cleanout door has been cleaned of the excess soot brushed down from the top. That is easy enough to do—locate the door near the bottom of the chimney and unlatch it. Use a flashlight to check the gook level. Hopefully it is clean. If it isn't, and the sweep was just there, the sweep didn't finish the job. Cleaning out the bottom of the chimney is part of the job. If it isn't done, get a small shovel, a pair of work gloves, a paper bag, preferably a face mask for you, and clean that mess out of there! Then find another sweep.

If you haven't had the chimney swept for awhile, and there is a pile of gook—call that sweep immediately. To be really clever, and check between sweepings yourself, use a small mirror and your flashlight to shine the light up the chimney to inspect it yourself. This you should do anyway. Or ask your sweep to show you how.

Check it yourself

Using a mirror and flashlight, look for cracks, obstacles (bird or animal nests) and other things that don't belong there. If you find something, don't use the chimney until it has been cleaned out first.

Chimneys made of chimney block, a one-piece square doughnut block stacked up, are inherently dangerous. If one of these chimneys does crack, get a proper chimney built to replace it, using at least 4" block and *shiplap* or overlapping flues with insulation in the cavity between the flues and the block. Or, have a stainless-steel liner installed within a 4" block chimney. If possible, have the chimney surrounded with brick around the basic block. That's one of the safest chimneys around.

If your chimney doesn't have a flueliner, get it lined before you use it.

An architect built a house using 4,000 cement bricks on the outside of the house instead of normal brick, as a "design element." To keep the proper "design element" intact, the bricks weren't waterproofed. Every rainstorm, 4,000 "sponges" sucked in rain and dumped it into the house. Finally, the insurance company got tired of replacing the carpets! The chimney was waterproofed by stuccoing it properly.

Cracks

Cracks that are larger than hairline, can be dangerous. Here you'll need an expert mason's help and advice. Find out what caused the cracks in the first place. Was it a chimney fire earlier? Is there rubble between the flueliner and the outside walls of the chimney? Are there flueliners (don't laugh, very early chimneys didn't have them)?

The rubble issue is an interesting one. Many masons use the busted bricks and junk (soda cans and debris) to fill the space between the flues and the walls of the chimney. As the fireplace or woodstove is used and heats up the chimney, the chimney expands. As the fire dies down, the whole mess settles. When this settles down, the now colder, more compacted rubble can push the sides of the chimney out and crack the walls. The solution is to rebuild the chimney without the rubble and with a proper insulated flue system (stainless steel is an excellent choice).

Have a qualified chimney sweep do his/her job cleaning it at the end of the season and before the season starts again.

Spalling

When water gets into the bricks and later freezes, it pops the bricks apart. This is an indication that the bricks are "soft" brick, as are many "used" brick. Used brick should only be used inside a structure, not outside. They do need to be protected from the elements—because of the ability of water to penetrate beyond the surface. Quite simply, the bricks outside the house should be replaced. If you have used brick and like the look, there are newer hard bricks that look almost exactly the same to the untrained eye. Spalling brick undermines the integrity of the structure. Until the situation is examined by an expert mason, leave the chimney alone—don't use it. The outside portion of the chimney, if it is compromised, may have to be replaced.

Another cause of spalling is "raked" joints. If the joints are cleaned out and about ¼" inside the edge of the brick, the mason literally raked or cleaned out the mortar between the bricks. This leaves a ledge for snow, water

Cost Effective

A safe chimney adds to the value of your house when you decide to sell it.

Check It!

Check for cracks, or lines running up the length of the chimney. Look for loose bricks, mortar, bits or pieces of bricks lying around the base of the chimney.

Spalling
A brick has popped out of the chimney. You can see the bits of brick on the roof. That metal stuff is the lead flashing used to prevent water getting between the chimney and the roof.

and problems to develop. It allows a grand entrance into the chimney. As this method, while an interesting design element used quite frequently, doesn't firmly squish the mortar tight, it allows water inside the brick through the joints. The water freezes in winter, cracks the brick, and soon, bits of brick are all over your lawn. The best joints are the type that are almost flush with the brick and squashed in with a jointing tool.

Loose bricks or mortar

Something is fundamentally wrong with your chimney if the bricks and/or mortar are raining on you. Don't use it until you have it inspected by a qualified mason. The structure is unstable and potentially dangerous. Keep kids and pets away from it. Deal with it *now!*

Causes can be acid from the smoke eating out the mortar, water damage, or lack of flueliner. If you look in your clean-out door (presuming you have one at the bottom of the chimney) you might see lots of sand. That is part of the dead mortar which is made with sand. You have a serious problem. Have it looked into as soon as possible.

Chimney flashing (leaks)

Flashing should be tight to the structure of the house. It is usually copper or lead attached to the chimney, and aluminum is commonly found on the house part. Sometimes when using different types of flashing together, their chemical makeup clashes and eats each other away. It is better when all the flashing material is the same material. Peter's experience with flashing is that aluminum should never be used in the chimney itself. Mortar eats the aluminum away.

The flashing should be flush to the roof. Small flaps in the flashing can be fixed using a *small* dab of roofing cement to anchor the flap back in place.

Leaks through the flashing have to be dealt with immediately, before you have to replace your roof or parts of it. There are two layers of flashing. The first is put in by the mason while building the chimney, attached to the chimney itself. The second is installed by the roofing contractor as part of the roof and slipped under the chimney flashing. Depending on which flashing is causing the problem, whom do you call? You need to check for leaks around the chimney where it comes into the house—at the top.

If you use quality contractors, neither will wreck the other's flashing job. It will be done correctly. If one of the contractors doesn't know what he is doing, something will go wrong and plenty of time will pass, along with the water damage while you try to track down "whodunit" and who is going to fix it.

If water is drooling in, the cause can be one of several:

√ water has saturated the brick structure
√ the flashing has failed somewhere—also check to see if the water is wicking away from the chimney along the underneath of the roof
√ a crack in the chimney, chimney cap, or joints

Obviously, leaks from the chimney are masonry related—call the mason. Leaks from *flashing* could be either mason or roofer. Usually a good contractor will come to investigate the situation and tell you honestly what needs to be done—whether it is his/her job or the other contractor's job. If you call the mason and he/she tells you it's the roofers' job and you don't know a roofer, ask for the mason's recommendation as they often work together and know each other's work.

Dampers—fireplaces

Most dampers in fireplaces are inside the fireplace itself, just up above where the air gets sucked into the chimney. There is a big handle inside of the fireplace used to open and close it. Obviously, you must open it when you start a fire, and close it when the fire is completely out. If the damper gets knocked out of alignment (during sweeping or perhaps by an over-energetic attempt to open it), it needs to be put back in place.

Check it! If you have an attic, take a flashlight with you and check the roof around the chimney. If it is dry and cozy, nothing chipping away—no problem with the chimney.

Dampers can be damaged beyond reasonable repair. Don't sweat it. Have a mason or sweep install a top damper. They aren't expensive and actually may help your chimney survive longer as they prevent animals, birds, rain, snow and other stuff from getting into the chimney itself. A long chain from the fireplace to the damper is used to open and shut it. There are several types, so ask your installer what he/she recommends.

Drafts

Closed houses only have so much air inside them. When we breathe, we use up air. When a fireplace is lit, it too, needs air to survive. The bigger the fireplace, the more air it needs to draw from the house. The more airtight the house, the bigger this problem becomes.

When you light a fire in your fireplace, does it draw properly? Does the smoke go up the chimney? Or into the house?

If "into the house" is the answer, you need more air to make the chimney draw the smoke up and out. So many houses nowadays are built so "airtight" that there isn't enough air to allow a chimney to draw properly. One way to check this is to crack a window in the same room to allow the air in. If the chimney starts drawing well—there's your answer.

To permanently correct this problem, an outside air inlet can be installed by a mason—if there isn't one installed (and working) already.

If there is an outside air inlet installed, perhaps the fireplace is just too big for the chimney. This does happen. To rectify this problem, the fireplace has to be "made smaller" somehow. One way is to lower the height of the fireplace opening. Call a trusted mason. This isn't a DIY job.

Roofs

There are many ruins in Scotland, shells of old stone houses left behind once the roof was gone. It was better to abandon the house than try to repair it. Without a roof, your house is useless. It is far better to put extra effort into keeping it up than trying to repair neglect later.

Please, don't go for cheap here. Having the best contractor, one specializing in roofing with a sound reputation, may cost a bit more initially, but will save you big in the long run. They are the ones who can completely redo your roof in a day or two—and not diddle around, costing you more and more money in the end. An incompetent roofer can leave you with a leaking roof—something you were trying to prevent in the first place!

In cold climates ice can build up onto the roof and under shingles destroying them, so check for ice damage, most noticeable along the edges of roofs. You'll see shingles or edges shoved up or out of alignment. It would probably be best to have a roofing pro fix the roof.

Check for moss, algae and other forms of weird things growing on your roof. Overhanging limbs hiding the sun, humid or damp conditions, lack of air circulation—all can aid in growing foreign roof eaters. There are products made for this. As the chemicals are toxic, it would be better to have your roofing pro handle the job unless you are quite comfortable with messing around with this stuff yourself. You'll need some type of protection for yourself while you mess with the chemicals. The products can be found at hardware and home supply stores.

Asphalt shingles

What you look for depends on what type of roof you have. Shingles and shakes are common roofing materials. Asphalt shingles last an average of 10–25 years depending on the quality of the shingles. When you see corners of asphalt shingles missing, loose, out of line, or curled up—find a good roofing contractor. If the actual roof itself is in seriously bad shape, you may have to replace the entire roof. If you are vigilant, the "repair" can be as simple as putting on another layer of shingles.

Check it

Look for any changes since your last inspection. If you can't see your roof well, if there are any neighboring houses, ask your neighbor if you can look at your roof from one of their windows.

Ice Dams

If you find ice dam damage, have the ventilation checked in the roof itself. There should be air flowing through the underside of the roof—keeping the roof itself cold, and the heat inside the house—not melting the snow on the roof.

Ridge vents

These need to be clear of debris— things like pine needles, leaves, twigs and the like. If they get blocked, your roof won't be adequately vented possibly leading to problems later. Make sure they stay clean and clear.

Rust streaks

can indicate damage underneath the roof itself. If the streaks come from a chimney, that has to be investigated for chimney leaks.

Wood shakes

Because wooden shake shingles are so beautiful, too many houses in wooded areas use this material. Unfortunately, they burn just as beautifully during a forest fire, often setting a house on fire that wouldn't necessarily have burned otherwise. If you live in an area that has been or can be threatened by forest fires, find out what you need to do if the threat becomes reality. Is there a fire retardant which could be used on the shakes? Even better, can it be used *now* instead of later to prevent a fire?

In the meantime, look for broken, split or loose shakes. Have them repaired as soon as you can. While the repair is being done, have the roofer look for underlying damage, just in case. It is better to get that taken care of at the same time, instead of waiting until the roof caves in.

Tile

Look for cracked tiles. These should be replaced as soon as practical. Loose ones need to be put back in place, or replaced if necessary. If there is an underlying cause for the damage, have it taken care of at the same time.

Metal

These little dears can rust. They can also bend. And tear. Wee holes can be repaired with a version of a Wet Surface Roof Cement troweled on evenly. But that is just a quickie "holding" solution. A better solution? Have the roof properly repaired.

Gutters

There are several types of gutter material: plastic, aluminum, steel, copper, seamless metal. The gutter directs water away from the foundation to safe places to prevent water build-up around the foundation—and therefore, wet or leaking basements and crawl spaces.

Unless you have some sort of gutter guard system over the gutter to keep out stray leaves and other junk and you know the gutter is perfect, grab a ladder and something to run along the inside of the gutter and clean it out. (We have used an old paint roller and handle on an extension pole to reach some of our gutters.) If you can't do it, hire someone.

- ⮞ Check the gutters for any damage. It will have to be repaired quickly.

- ⮞ Look in any corners or joints for leaks.

- ⮞ Check the downspouts to make sure they are sound.

- ⮞ Are there any holes along the length?

- ⮞ Watch for rust holes.

A piece of bent rebar used to push pine needles and leaves out of a gutter.

- ⮞ Most important, make sure the gutter is still leading *down* to the downspout. The gutter shouldn't be absolutely straight, or the water has nowhere to go. It needs to be heading down at least ¼" for every 4 feet of length towards the downspout. If the gutter is sagging, it could be because something holding the gutter to the house has failed, or broken. If it isn't your bag to fix it—hire someone to do it for you.

Siding

Protecting your siding, no matter what it is made of, is critical. It is protecting you and your house from the elements. The purpose of siding is to ventilate the outside walls, to prevent water penetration of the structure, and protect the house from the elements.

Blistering paint

Paint gets old and wears out. Just think of the work it does to protect you and your house! Usually, blistering paint means something underneath isn't working correctly. Perhaps the wood is rotting due to moisture invasion, or the primer coat wasn't good enough to last, or worse, nobody "back painted" the siding before it was installed. All sides and edges of siding must be painted before installation. If it wasn't done, that's a good "probable" of the cause.

Clean it!
Gutters should be cleaned out once a year.

To prevent blistering paint, prime clean wood siding before you paint or stain it.

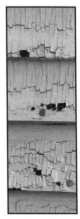

Paint

If you do it right the first time, with a reputable painting contractor, and the best paints, you will have a paint job that will last for years.

If your house is painted, make sure you go for the best paint available—don't throw away good money on a bad paint job. What you save initially you will more than pay for when you have to repaint it again—and scrape all that junk paint off first.

Rotting

Rotted siding needs to be replaced and quickly. It would help to find out why the siding rotted in the first place. Is there water damage? Sun damage? Your best bet is to find a reliable contractor whose team can come in and do the repair job quickly. Your house can't afford to be exposed to the elements for long. Unreliable contractors or DIY jobs can leave the house exposed to more damage in the future.

Cracks, buckling and dents

If cracks, dents or buckling are letting the elements into your house structure, get a contractor to replace the affected parts as soon as practical and find out what caused the damage in the first place, then rectify the problem.

Aluminum or vinyl siding dented?

Can you live with it? Then don't worry about it—and tell the kids to play ball elsewhere.

If you have some extra of the product used on your house, and wish to replace it yourself, proceed carefully as it isn't easy to work with. Do *not* pound the nails tight against the siding as the siding needs to expand and contract with the heat and cold weather. This is best handled by a pro.

Nail popping

If you find nails popping, it could be that the under structure is rotting, therefore the nails don't hold anymore. Or the wrong nails were used, in which case take them out and use the proper nails for the job. Perhaps the siding is buckling or expanding—why? Is moisture affecting it? Get it taken care of by a pro before more damage is done.

Shriveling wood siding

Much sun damage is caused by dark-colored paints and/or stains on wood. As the sun heats it up, the wood dries, and dries, and shrinks. When the situation gets to the point that the siding isn't doing its job, it will have to be replaced. To prevent that in the future, either use light-colored paints or stains, or perhaps, build an overhang to keep the sun off that wall.

Some of this damage could be caused by moisture—either the siding wasn't kiln dried completely, or water got into the siding. If the situation is causing problems with the structure of the house, get the siding replaced. Check for underlying problems behind the initial damage and have that fixed.

Cracks in brick veneer

However, cracks can lead to water damage (what else!) behind the walls. Hairline cracks shouldn't be a worry. Anything big enough to allow water through is a worry, could be structural and should be looked at by a mason as soon as possible.

Water penetration

This is serious business. Anytime water gets behind the siding, you have a problem. Rather than fuss with it, find a contractor who can stop the water problem immediately. The source of the problem may not be obvious.

Laundry Room

If yours is like mine, it's a "dash-down-and-get-the-job-over-with" sort of place. Many are finished and look great all the time. If yours is unfinished, all this is easier to check. If the room is finished, you'll have to simply look for signs of water leaks in the ceilings and walls.

Check pipes

Water pipes sweat and drip. They can also leak like crazy. Sweating and dripping is normal in humid conditions. Wrapping the pipe with insulation (3' long black foam sections that slip over the water pipes and get taped into place) will solve that problem. If the problem is a leak—call your plumber immediately.

Veneer brick
Generally speaking, veneer brick walls are not weight-bearing walls, but are used as an outer protection.

Water heater

Water heaters should never be set higher than 120 degrees unless you have a darned good reason to do so. Hotter water can burn you or your children quickly. You can check the temperature yourself and set it to 120°F. Most newer dishwashers heat the water for you, so you don't need to set the water heater any higher for that purpose.

Electric

The issue with electric water heaters is the heating elements themselves. They get covered with calcium and lime deposits. The more deposited on the heating elements, the harder the water heater has to work to heat the water—costing you money. There are usually two elements, one high and one low near the bottom. Sediment builds up around the lower element making it even harder for it to work properly. The recommendation from the heating professionals is to hook up a hose to the faucet on the bottom and empty a couple of quarts of water into a pan or bucket to clean out that sediment. Once a year should be fine unless lots of junk comes out—then do it every month or so until it runs clear.

Gas

When you first moved in, you should have had the gas company send someone over to check out your gas appliances. If not, have someone come over and tell you about your heater. Ask them what you can and can't do with it. Gas is dangerous stuff.

Check furnace

Every year, *without fail*, your furnace (if you have one) must be cleaned, filters changed, and completely inspected by a competent plumbing and heating contractor or your fuel supplier. Hopefully, when you bought your house, part of the information given you was who installed your furnace. Start there.

Vital Info

All water heaters come with paperwork telling you what you can and can't do for yours.

Read it!

If you didn't get any papers with it, call the manufacturer and ask the company to send you the appropriate papers. Have the model number with you when you call. It can be found on the unit front and center.

Check vents and clear

If there are any other vents leading out of your basement, make sure they are clear of debris, and any flaps can flap properly. Blockage can be a serious threat to your house. Gases can back up and kill you. If you have any questions concerning vents, call the company you have chosen to maintain the equipment.

Clean dryer vents and hoses

Watch for kinks in the hose. Absolute no-no. You don't want anything to hamper the airflow, thus making a spot for lint to gather, clot and eventually burn.

Dryer vents have a nasty habit of getting clogged with lint. Not just the lint collector in the dryer but the hoses leading out of the house as well. Outside, find the vent housing and open it. If it looks clean, you are way ahead. If it is a mess, start cleaning the lint out. Then do the same with the inside end. Most vent hoses are collapsible making it fairly easy to check and clean the whole thing out. When done, replace it the way you found it—making sure there aren't any kinks or tight corners or folds in the hose.

If it is really a disgusting mess, opt for a new hose. They are easily purchased (and not expensive) from a hardware store. Have an idea of how long the hose is before you buy a replacement. If the distance between the wall outlet and the dryer is minimal, not to worry. You can install it yourself. You may have to move your dryer out of the way to get to the hose. (They aren't heavy—if you need help, grab another willing body, the stronger the better.) Usually, it's a matter of pulling out the hose from the dryer and sticking the new hose in its place. Same with the end going out of the house.

Check carbon monoxide detector

There should be a test button on the detector. Test it and change the battery at least once a year, if it uses one. Make sure the unit itself is working properly. There are some that simply don't work. Replace it if yours is one of those.

Heads UP
Most water heaters come set for 140°F. You can and should change that down to 120°F for your own safety. Just note that some states are now requiring water heaters to be set at 140°F due to a "possibility" of Legionnaire's Disease.

Attics

If you have an unfinished attic, this is for you. There may be spaces around a finished top floor that are attic storage. Check these out as well.

Check outside venting and clear

Ventilation in attics is critical. Air needs to flow around and through the attic space to keep the attic dry, the roof dry, and to keep the attic from overheating. Make sure any vents or screens are clear of nests, dirt, debris, stored items and anything hindering air flow.

Check insulation and repair

The insulation should be even and clean. Watch for little animals building nests and get rid of them. Fill in the spaces created by the nest.

Make sure the insulation isn't pulling away from the joists and is tight. You don't want any gaps. There should be a way for air to vent from the edges of the actual box of the walls down the roof to the outside. Usually, there are foam channels along this route to make sure the air gets through.

Check for water damage on roof decking

While you are up here (as you read in the chimney part) check for water spots and damage. If you find any, get them taken care of immediately! Call your roofing pro and have them send one of their estimators out and look at your roof.

Chapter 12

Energy Efficiency

Do you want to save some serious money? Without changing your lifestyle appreciably? It isn't that hard to do. Even the most simple adjustments make a huge difference.

I highly recommend *The Home Energy Diet* by Paul Scheckel (ISBN 978-0-86571-530-0 $18.95 New Society Publishers) if you wish to delve into this more seriously. Paul takes you through a complete audit of where and how to save money, while being energy smart—without giving up your lifestyle.

Take your electric bill for example

Did you know that if you shut down—completely—your home computer, and television sets, including the cable boxes, VCRs, DVD players and the like, you could potentially save enough on your electric bill to pay for a month or more of service on your cable bill?

Many appliances have a "stand-by" mode that uses electricity even when you don't think it is. Cable boxes, DVD and VCRs, radios, anything with a built-in clock. Some of these can be shut-off without affecting how it is used by you. Others, well, those clocks do come in handy.

We borrowed a watt meter from Efficiency Vermont to test our appliances and usage. We thought we were really doing well as we only used between 400–600

Shut it OFF Of course, shutting off lights and/or appliances you aren't using saves energy. No sense in paying for something you aren't using.

Energy Efficiency

kilowatts (kWh) a month. When I spoke with Li Ling Young, Project Manager of Efficiency Vermont and told her what our usage was, she told me her usage was about 200 kWh a month.

After metering a few days on several appliances and television setups, we came to these Daily Costs for just four appliances, and here's what we did about it:

Appliance	Daily cost	Yearly cost	After changes	Savings	Difference or changes
chest freezer	$ 0.25	$ 91.25	$ 28.00	$ 63.25	New Energy-Star version
TV and cable	$ 0.31	$112.42	$ 60.00	$ 52.42	Shutting off all power
22-cf fridge	$ 0.32	$116.80	$ 34.00	$ 82.80	New Energy-Star version
computer system	$ 1.00	$365.00	$275.00	$ 90.00	Shutting off all power when not used

Total saved on just these four steps: $288.47 a year, or roughly 2,219 kWh/year. Still over the 200 kwh a month, but getting there. Vermont's electric rates (currently $.13+/kWh) are some of the highest in the country, so this is significant savings for us.

The changes? We promptly replaced the chest freezer with a 7.5-cubic foot Energy Star version and dropped that cost to $28/year. We had already replaced the dying 1987-vintage 22-cubic foot refrigerator (at $117/year) with an Energy Star bottom-freezer model that cost $34/year to run.

To deal with the expense of the television setup, we have all the plugs on a surge protector, and shut that off when we go to bed. That shuts off the cable box, television and everything else. Saves us about one-third to one-half the expense of running the television for the few hours it is on—or about one month's cable bill. With two television sets and cable boxes, shutting them off saves another month on the bill.

As to the computer setup? I use my computer for my business. I run it up to 16 hours a day. But if I leave it for a few hours, I now shut it down, and shut it down for the night, completely shutting off any power to external peripherals (printers, and such), the monitor, and the modems via surge protectors and a UPS (uninterruptible power source).

Consider UPS protectors are invaluable devices and highly recommended even for *all* electronics.

When the next electric bill came after making some of these changes, our usage dropped by 98 kWh from the same period the year before, and the bill dropped by $6. With a rate hike of over 9% looming, that savings will add up.

Here's the difference in three months of electric bills over two summers in Vermont. In both Augusts, we ran a dehumidifier in one large basement room that worked for the entire basement. The difference in electric rates is due to 2005's rate structure (if you use over 500 kWh/month, you paid a bit less), then rate increases for 2006.

Month	2005 kWh	Cost / kWh	Our Bill	2006 kWh	Cost / kWh	Our Bill
July	467	0.138	$66.38	491	0.136	$68.86
Aug	585*	0.133	$80.25	433	0.139	$62.26
Sept	480	0.138	$67.91	382	0.142	$55.99

*The increase is due to running a dehumidifier most of the month of August.

Saving 2,219 kWh may not seem like much to you, but multiplied by thousands of other homes doing the same, that would save this country a fortune in power consumption and fossil fuels. Not to mention the cost of building more power plants or ruining more pristine places looking for a finite supply of fuel.

Other ways to save

Lighting
Exchange the light bulbs in your frequently used lamps to compact fluorescent lamps (CFL). We have already.

Not only do they last longer, but the cost to run them, using 1/4 to 1/3 the power, more than makes up for their initial expense. However, in many cases the initial expense is offset by immediate rebates. If you don't get a rebate certificate from the store, check with your power company.

Better
The new CFL bulbs are smaller and better quality than the first ones sold. Look for rebates where you purchase them.

Where practical, install fluorescent lights in high use areas. The newer fixtures use electronic ballasts, rather than the old magnetic ballasts, so they don't flicker and drive you crazy anymore.

Fluorescent bulbs and anything else containing mercury needs to be treated as hazardous waste. It is being collected and recycled. Look for a location near you through your local hardware stores or waste collection facility.

Computers

Think about your computer at work—you may use it 8 hours a day, 5 days a week, but if you leave it on constantly, you are using the computer only 23.8% of the time it is on, yet it is using power another 128 hours a week! My computer system costs me about $1 a day even when I do shut it down—if I don't turn off all the components at the power strip. Imagine the cost when you don't. And how many power plants have to be built to power the computers left on 24/7.

The reason computers were left on 24/7 in the "old days" was to protect the power supply. Turning a computer on sends a surge of current through the unit that eventually blows out the computer's power supply. But in this day and age, who keeps a computer long enough for that to happen anyway? It takes years of use and most computers are replaced every two to three years.

Please—if you are leaving your computer for more than one hour—turn it off—all the way down to the power strips. Not only are you saving money, but you are protecting your computer from being hacked if you happen to have a high-speed connection. There are programs anyone can buy or download that allow anyone access to a "turned-off" computer that not only turns on the computer, but allows it to be used, or hacked. Unless, there isn't any power to the computer—period.

Clothes washer

The quickest way to save is to use only cold water, saving the cost of water heating. There are plenty of choices of detergents formulated for cold water use.

If you are buying a new washer, get a front-loading washer. They are much more efficient, use less water, and are more effective at cleaning!

Clothes dryers

If you can skip the dryer and hang your clothes to dry outside (you don't want the moisture inside your house, especially in the basement), do so. It will save you a bundle.

Coffee makers

If you make a big pot of coffee and leave the coffee maker on to keep the pot warm, you are using anywhere from 800–1,000 watts of electric to do so. That's a heck of a lot of power cycling on and off. Instead, to keep your coffee warm, put it in a thermal carafe. And unplug the coffee maker.

Dishwashers

Use only the "air dry" setting, rather than heat drying your dishes. And only wash full loads. No need to boost the water heater's temperature to help the dishwasher, it does it by itself.

Clear the filter of food bits at the bottom of the machine frequently. It is supposed to be done once a month or so.

Use the least amount of detergent needed to get the job done, and only run full loads. A study conducted by the University of Bonn, Germany found that washing dishes by hand used up more water and energy than running a dishwasher. Washing a 12-place setting by

T'ain't Trash! Don't throw away an old computer, recycle it!

Warning! Make sure the dryer vent hose is clean of lint, and clean the lint filter with each load. A blocked vent hose is a fire hazard waiting to happen, not only a money waster.

hand used an average of 27 gallons of hot water and 2.5 kWh of energy, whereas the dishwasher used only 4 gallons of water and 1.5 kWh of energy. Not only that, but the about half the hand-washed dishes were judged not fit to place on a table, they were so dirty!

Range hood

Be careful using one of these if you have the type that vents to the outside. It is designed to suck air out of the house. But where will the air come from? Be careful you don't suck out all your heat in the winter and have a source of incoming replacement air. If your vent's location isn't placed properly (too close to the furnace exhaust chimney), the range vent could be sucking furnace exhaust back into house. This is a potentially fatal problem.

Recycle!

If you are replacing an appliance—recycle it!

If you need extra air to run a powerful kitchen vent, open a window slightly to supply the needed air.

Anything gas-powered: If you see much yellow in the flame, call for a service tech quickly. The appliance isn't burning efficiently!

Do-It List

- Unplug unused appliances
- Replace incandescent bulbs with CFLs
- Put media (TV, DVD, etc.) on power strips and shut off when not being used
- Turn off lights not being used
- Recycle what can be recycled
- Compost what can be composted

Chapter 13

Going Green, Going Healthy

In this day and age, saving money can also mean saving the environment and your health. The more chemicals we consumers use, to more chemicals we are exposed. Looking at the health picture these days, with soaring rates of asthma, cancer and other ills, it behooves us to clean up our own environment—our lifestyle, our homes, and our property.

Cleaning "green"

This isn't difficult. It could be as easy as using different cleaners. It isn't necessary to kill all the germs in your life. Too sterile an environment isn't always healthy, either.

Here's an example from a friend, a WWII prison camp survivor:

> Joostien was pregnant with her third child when she and her two children were imprisoned in the camps in southeast Asia. She was a "clean freak"—her children were as spotless as possible under the conditions. But, she and her children were constantly ill. This was in contrast the family in the next hovel. Those children played in the dirt and mud, and cleanliness wasn't emphasized. After several rounds of illnesses and almost losing one of her children, Joostien asked her neighbor why her children were so healthy, and Joostien's

Non-Toxic
There is a difference between a "spotlessly clean" toxic home, and a clean, but non-toxic home.

Effective?
What research findings show is only bleach cleaned up bacteria, but only momentarily.

weren't. Her neighbor's answer was simple: *When her children played in the dirt (their environment) they became immune to the germs.* Joostein gave up the "clean routine." She and her three children survived the years of captivity healthy.

Antibacterial soaps and other products are not doing anything good for our environment. They aren't keeping you healthier, either. A study in the *Annals of Internal Medicine* reported in March 2, 2004 on a double-blind study that shows antibacterial products don't make a difference in the level of sickness in families using products containing antibacterial ingredients, or those who don't. The Findings Summary states: *"Antibacterial household cleaning products do not seem to reduce the number of infections among household residents, an expected finding because viruses, not bacteria, account for most household infections."*[1]

Windows!
Want the cleanest windows in town? Use white vinegar in water and spray it on your windows. Wipe the window down with a microfiber cloth. It's much faster than alternatives.

So why introduce more unneeded chemicals into your home?

Many of these chemicals are altering your own health in unexpected ways. *The Savvy Woman's Health Guide™ Series* has several books that will open your eyes to the effects of "excitotoxins" on your environment and your health—particularly women's and children's health.

Alternative cleaners

If you want to live a healthier life, try using microfiber cloths to clean—they don't require anything more than water, or water and white vinegar to do the job. From windows, mirrors to countertops and floors, these cloths are amazing cleaners. And to clean them, just toss them in the washing machine and reuse them. They are available everywhere.

[1] "Effect of Antibacterial Home Cleaning and Handwashing Products on Infectious Disease Symptoms. A Randomized, Double-Blind Trial." It is in the 2 March 2004 issue of Annals of Internal Medicine (volume 140, pages 321–329). The authors are E.L. Larson, S.X. Lin, C. Gomez-Pichardo, and P. Della-Latta.

I have white kitchen cabinets, and terra cotta tile countertops and floor. A quick swipe with a damp microfiber cloth and the whole place looks new. If the dirt is too bad, white vinegar cleans up the mess quickly. I have to mention we have 4 dogs, 2 cats, and live at the end of a dirt road in wetland territory. If you don't think that's a recipe for dirt, it's a constant. Add to that the woodstove we heat with in cold weather.

Are you poisoning yourself?

I threw out my collection of lethal chemicals. Some of them had to go to the hazardous waste collection in town! Imagine using hydrochloric acid to clean a toilet. White vinegar does very well indeed. Just brush around the bowl, and leave it in overnight. I've even added it to the tank awaiting the next flush.

Or, try one of the organic products made with essential oils. There are quite a few "green" product companies offering a myriad of products. Even some of the major companies are offering recycled and/or "green" products. While they may be a bit more expensive than the products you are used to using, the cost to your health is significantly less. Have a look at the products from Seventh Generation based in Burlington, Vermont. Their website has a terrific downloadable booklet on toxins in your home, and what to do about it. In fact, many major companies are getting the message from consumers and recycled products are becoming more common.

When it comes to your lawn

The Toxics Action Center of New England, based in Boston, with offices in four New England states, has been documenting toxic waste sites throughout the area, among other issues affecting our long-term health. Their findings are shocking. If you don't think the situation is pervasive, think again.

Super cleaner
Vermont Soap makes *Liquid Sunshine* that really does clean just about anything, safely!
vermontsoap.com

Do the research!
Have you ever checked the Manufacturer's Safety Data Sheets (MSDS) on some of the products you use? Check a products website for the information.

There are other ways to grow grass. This is just one of many areas where you can make a difference in your environment and your health. This news release is used with their permission:

> A report completed by Toxics Action Center, a New England-wide environmental and public health organization, revealed the disturbing truth about the toxins used by TruGreen ChemLawn.

> Using the pesticide manufacture's Material Safety Data Sheets and peer reviewed scientific studies, Toxics Action Center found that their chemicals have been proven to threaten our health, and disturbingly, our children are particularly vulnerable to these toxins. The report can be found at www.toxicsaction.org.

> Scientific studies associate exposure to the pesticides used by ChemLawn with a whole host of human health problems including asthma, cancer, reproductive problems, birth defects and disruption of the hormonal system.

> Among many other alarming findings, children exposed to weed killers early in life are four and a half times more likely to develop asthma. A study published in the Journal of the National Cancer Institute found that household and garden pesticide use can increase the risk of childhood leukemia as much as seven-fold. 2,4-D, one of ChemLawn's pesticides, is linked by scientific studies to Non-Hodgkin's lymphoma. Pesticides can also cause reproductive problems such as infertility, miscarriages, and birth defects.

> Once ChemLawn sprays pesticides on a lawn they do not stay there. Babies play on the grass, and put things like dirt and grass in their mouths, ingesting the pesticides. Pesticides are tracked into homes on shoes where they get into the air and remain in carpet fibers for years. These toxic chemicals are now so ubiquitous they are now found in umbilical cord blood, and breast milk.

Toxic! Is a chemically created green lawn worth the risk to your health?

Chapter 14

Dealing with Pesky Things

Bugs is bugs. You may love them, you may hate the creepy things. Still, while some are good, quite a few aren't.

Not all spiders are bad. They eat bad bugs (as well as some good ones). They make a mess in your dark corners. Still, there are advantages to having spiders reside with you. And that is getting rid of the bad bugs.

Preventive Measures

If an unwanted critter can't get into your abode, then it can't wreak havoc within. Therein lies the problem. There is generally somewhere they can get in. You may not be able to see immediately where the pests are gaining entrance, but if you are plagued with ants, mice and other unwanted visitors, then they are getting in via their own private gateway.

Sealing entrances

The first thing to do is to figure out where they are getting in. Walk around your house and look very closely for holes, even minute ones, that a stream of ants or mice could use. You may notice marks on the foundation walls giving you a clue. Look around the ground for telltale signs of a trail. If the entrance has been used by one critter, it has been used by lots of them.

If you have a "stick" house, the most common is simply put: a wooden house built of "2 by 4s" (wood framing covered with wallboard on the inside) on top of a concrete or cement block foundation wall. Look along the bottom of the foundation, especially if it is close to the ground. Look along the sill plate—the piece of wood that lies along the top of the concrete or block foundation wall and the framing above.

Holes?

When you find a hole, seal it up—if at all possible.

Trouble is, if the critters want in, they can usually get in. You also have to gaze upwards to the roof. Little critters will and do climb right up your outside walls to the roof to gain entrance. A mouse only needs a space about the diameter of your little finger to get in. Are there any slat vent openings without a screen in your attic?

Losing contact

If there aren't any holes that you can see down below, and the critters can't get up the siding (vinyl and aluminum make it difficult), there could be another route. Check to see if any trees are touching the house. Trees are a perfect access route for squirrels, mice and other unwanted guests.

If there are branches offering a route, either tie them up out of the way, or cut off the end just far enough to prevent the interlopers from jumping across to your roof. If it isn't practical for you to do it, find someone who can.

Multi-legged variety

In the fall, the creatures come in for the warmth; in the spring and summer, for the food. If you keep food stuffs stored and sealed in air-tight containers, the food isn't enticing. They can't smell it or get to it. Clean up your countertops of spilled stuff—jams and jellies, or milk and juice. Anything with sugar in it just yells out to ants and other unpleasant visitors.

Another place they reside is log piles. Keep it some distance away, even if you have to walk carrying the burden. It may save your house some serious structural damage and you a lot of headaches dealing with the wretched bugs.

Ants

Your basic household garden ant can be dealt with by using the "ant hotels" sold at any hardware store. Place them strategically around the kitchen, behind and out of the way of humans, but along their routes: the back corners of the countertops, in the back of cabinets and the like.

Serious ant issues, i.e., fireants, infestations of carpenter ants and other types beyond the "ant hotel" require professional help—think termite control (see below)—same sort of issue. Look for the pros in the Yellow Pages or by asking neighbors and friends who may have had the same problem. The faster you can get the pros on the problem, the better the chances you have of saving your house.

Logs
If you have a pile of firewood awaiting the heating season, make sure it is not next to your house.

Roaches

Same goes for roaches, the roach hotel, strategically placed will help. Keeping your house clean of food scraps and inviting goodies, goes a long way to keeping them out. If you do find roaches, too many to handle, time to call in a pro. These guys are bad news. Believe it or not, roaches often come in with grocery packing cartons!

Termites & wood-chomping bugs

These wretched bugs come for the wood food anyway. Your house is a potential Garden of Eden—if they can get to it.

If you notice little tunnels built onto the side of your house, or hear munching inside the walls, at least investigate the situation. Whether it is carpenter ants, termites, or other bugs, you need to know exactly what is going on.

If you wish to learn more on termites, hit the internet. Or call the local university Entomology department. They can give you the ultimate earful. Call your local Extension service as they can also help you, or at least direct you to help. What should you do if you find termites or other wood-chomping bugs? Call the pros—*now!* Simple. Don't hesitate. Read Chapter 23—Finding a Contractor on the "how-to's" of selecting the right pros for the job. Termites must be dealt with immediately. Before you don't have a house left to think about.

Safety first

Whatever method you choose to rid your abode of bugs, make sure the chemicals don't poison your environment. Remember, you have to live the results for a long time.

Okay, okay, you do have some time to work this out and do it correctly. It is more important to get the right company to do the best job the first time.

There are several ways to deal with termites and other subterranean bugs. The old way was to bury bait every so many feet (20 or so) in a perimeter away from the house. That left 19 feet between baits for bugs to wander. Not always the most effective method.

However, more choices of effective methods have been developed in the few years, including spraying chemicals along the foundation of the house itself. Make sure whatever you pick is safe for the environment. Unfortunately, if you have a well, or a source of water nearby (pond, stream, etc.) you may not be able to use any of these systems as they are very toxic to wildlife as well.

You want to deal with a company that is licensed to control pests. Their pros are now known as pest management professionals and belong to the National Pest Management Association. More information is on their website in Resources.

- Ask if the company has at least one licensed pro on staff.
- Ask them what they do to kill off the pests and how it will affect you, the homeowner.

🐛 Is the chemical safe?

🐛 Will it get into your environment, i.e., air, water, ground (where children play)?

🐛 Will you have to leave your house?

🐛 How long does it take to be effective, how long does it last?

🐛 Are there any guarantees or warranties? Exactly what are they. Don't expect to be rid of bugs forever. If you are guaranteed "forever" look for another pest management professional's opinion. "Forever" is just about impossible to guarantee.

When you speak to a pro, you need to get a complete description of what the heck is going on "down there," or "inside" your home.

Here are the pointers:

1. Do you really have termite damage? Or is it just suspected or "conducive to termite infestations"?

2. Get a clear description of the damage and what can be done about it. Is it ongoing, as in still active, or has activity ceased. If you find any of the bugs, take some of the critters or their evidence to your state's extension service. They can steer you to the right help and advise you.

3. Is there an excessive moisture content in the wood of your home? This is conducive to bugs as well as a host of other issues, including fungi. If fungi is suspected, find yourself a professional to deal with it immediately. There is a new fungus growing in some states that can wreck a house in days.

4. Get a proposal that exactly spells out what will happen and when. Have it explained thoroughly. Is the company going to do any digging on your property? Or will they poke a sprayer down into the ground around the house? Don't settle for "termite treatment" on the contract. If you have any questions,

Research
Do some research on the Internet before you make your calls to pros. That way you have a good idea of what is available and which application would be better for your situation.

call your extension service again.

5. Know that there are laws and/or rules about how the treatments are handled and applied. For example, these chemicals can't be applied near cisterns or wells.

6. Warranty: what is covered, is there re-treatment if the original treatment doesn't completely work? What about secondary infestations? What about pre-existing conditions?

7. Don't take the first company that comes to estimate or judge your situation. Get several estimates before choosing the right contractor.

Bats in the attic?

Hang a light bulb (CFL?) in the attic (where it won't start a fire) to discourage bats. They don't like light.

Good Bugs

Not all bugs are bad. And low and behold, birds love to eat the bad ones, too. If you can, hang some bird feeders around and get the type of birdseed that encourages the birds in your neighborhood. Birds feast on mosquitoes (so do bats, and they are usually good guys as well).

If you find a ladybug or ladybird beetle (same thing), that's a good bug. These friends eat the bad bugs that eat your plants, and occasionally mildew!

Those little green lacewings? Also eats aphids, scales, thrips, mites and insect eggs.

Dragonflies, praying mantis, lightning bugs... all good friends of your backyard. Encourage them!

Good bats

Bats are very good creatures. If you have bats around your locale, you are lucky. They clean out mosquitoes, and other nasty bugs.

If you don't want them in your house—by all means get a bat house and put it away from your house in a dark area (the woods?).

Part IV

Emergencies—
911 and Beyond

Chapter 15

Get Out Alive!

In case of a fire emergency, there isn't any time to think. You must learn to react the right way instantly, instinctively. That's why you need to think out escape routes within your house—then practice how to do it. If there are children in the household, they have to be taught how to get out safely, too.

Remember: you only have about 60–120 *seconds* to get out of the house alive! You don't have time to go back for anything. Nor time to stop to get anything.

If you are practicing what this book preaches, about using fire extinguishers and smoke alarms, you've made a good start. If not, go back to Chapter 4—Safety and Sanity and start again.

Plan your escape routes

There should be at least two escape routes to each room. That shouldn't be too hard, as there are windows and doors. If you can't get out the door and down the hall, by all means, get out of the window.

Windows

But first there has to be a way out of the window safely—to get to the ground safely.

Get OUT!
You have less than 2 minutes to get out of a burning structure safely. That's how long it takes for a fire to get to "blow-out" status.

Get Out Alive!

If you have screens on the windows, make sure everyone can remove them. In the winter, avoid that problem altogether by removing the screens and storing them elsewhere.

If there are security bars on the windows, you had better have a way to remove them quickly. Make sure the bars release instantly in an emergency. If not, get a pro to correct the situation. Don't wait to do this. It is a priority.

If the windows are on the ground floor, getting out of an open window isn't too much of an issue. Unless there is something below the window that can hurt you—rocks, spiky plants, broken glass, that sort of thing. Or the "first floor" happens to be hanging over a precipice. If there are hazards below the windows planned for an escape, clean up the area and make it safe. Or find another way out.

When our children were quite little, we discovered that their bedroom windows stuck fast in the winter. Those wooden frames swelled so tightly that no one could move them without a jack hammer. If Peter or I couldn't get the window open when there wasn't an emergency, did we think the children could? Of course not. We replaced the windows with ones they could open. We had them practice opening the windows and moved their beds where it made it easier for them to do so. Do give some thought to this problem.

Escape from higher floors

The higher the floor, the greater the need for something to get down. There are window ladders that can be kept near a window in each room. Everyone has to learn how to open the box, attach the ladder to the window sill and drop it outside. A young child may have a problem with this. Then you have to get out the window and down a shaky, wiggly ladder that doesn't always offer a great foothold. As there are many different types of ladders, don't settle for the first one you see.

You want a ladder that:

- stands out from the wall, allowing you to get your foot onto the rungs
- holds several hundred pounds of weight at once— enough for at least two people
- has non-slip rungs
- is easy enough for young children to get it out the window and use it by themselves
- is easily stored for quick access in an emergency
- is easy to use

The pros suggestion is to keep the ladder under a bed, or other place, easily reached by the potential ladder user. Everyone should know how to use it—practice hooking the ladder to the window and throwing the ladder out the window so the braces are against the wall, not hanging out into space. Then practice going down the ladder. The last thing you want is someone to freeze in fright as they try to escape a burning building.

You might consider installing a special ladder on the side of the house. There is a great one made by Jomy which hides in a channel and looks like a drainpipe until the release at the top is pulled. The ladder and safety rail then drop down into place making a sure-footed escape route to the ground. It is perfectly safe to leave in place as no one can open it from the ground to use it to gain access into the house.

Map out your escape routes. Literally draw them out on paper. Then make sure they are practical. Are there any obstructions or limitations to the routes? Can everyone open the doors and windows? Are there fire extinguishers within reach along the route? Is the furniture arranged for easy escape?

Practice a fire drill

Twice a year, everyone should go through the motions of getting out of the house in an emergency.

Make a Plan to Escape!

Make a workable plan that everyone can practice and use. Everyone old enough to get out on their own must be practiced in all the possibilities for escape.

Crawl, don't slither, along the escape routes. The deadly gases are hovering along the floor itself as well as just above "crawling head" level. After you've tried it a few times with your eyes open, try it blindfolded—as the situation will be during a real fire. Real fires turn everything black. You can't see anything, the fire pros can't see anything. That's why they practice so often. The smoke is so thick and so brutal that getting out quickly is your only hope of survival.

Don't pause to grab anything. Period. Too many people have died going back into buildings looking for someone who was already out. If everyone is trained to get out on their own (except, of course, the too tiny and too infirm), there isn't any need to go looking for someone else.

If you have to grab a small child, make sure you can escape from his/her room safely. If the child's room is next to yours, that's a help. The doors to our children's rooms were literally next to ours making any necessary rescue within the one minute time frame for a fire.

Teach everyone how to test a door before opening it. If it is hot, the fire is too close to the other side—don't open the door! If the door is cool or cold, it is probably safe to open.

If you can't open the door because of the intense heat, then stuff something in the crack to keep the smoke from getting into your room. It also keeps the window air from fanning the fire even more when you open the window.

Keep a cordless phone next to your bed for emergencies and grab it as you get up. Don't go looking for it if it isn't there. You'll waste precious time.

STOP, DROP, ROLL

Everyone should know the Stop, Drop, and Roll drill. If you or someone catches on fire STOP! Don't run and fan the flames. DROP to the ground and ROLL to extinguish the flames. Cover your face while doing this to protect your face and lungs from the fire and smoke. It does work.

Decals

Make sure each child's room has a sticker in the window showing the firemen where children can be found so they don't spend time fruitlessly searching. Have one on the front door telling the firemen about pets inside.

Kids are taught this at school from kindergarten on—or should be. It has saved many a child's life.

If you see someone else running while burning, stop them, make them drop and roll them to put out the flames.

Fire extinguishers and how to use them

After having read Chapter 4—Safety and Sanity, you should have plenty of the correct types of fire extinguishers around your home.

The time to seriously read the directions is well before you need to use the equipment. If you haven't boned up on their use, do it. Make it instinctive: know where they are located, grab one, yank the pin, aim the hose—and *squeeze* the trigger.

To make it easy for you, this is the way to remember how to use an extinguisher:

Pull the pin on the extinguisher

Aim the extinguisher hose at the BASE of the fire

Squeeze the handle

Sweep the extinguisher back and forth along the base of the fire to completely cover the base

WARNING
Do *not ever* go back into a burning house! *NEVER!*

If you have the rechargeable extinguishers, have them inspected and recharged as per the schedule on the unit itself. The little indicator on every extinguisher should be in the green area, meaning it is ready to use.

Once the extinguisher has been used—if it is a rechargeable one, then get it recharged. If it is a one-time-use only, heave it in the trash—after discharging the entire unit. You can tell the difference between the one-time use and the rechargeable: the one-timers have plastic tops and handles, the reusables use metal for the tops and handles.

Have a meeting place outside the house

Very important—have a place where everyone can meet, once they are out, and get counted! The meeting place must be safely away from the fire and easy to get to. It must be a place where firemen can readily find you to count heads and ask any questions. And it must be a place that won't be in the way of the firemen while they are working.

Smart Idea
Ask your local fire department for decals and any advice they could give you. They would probably be happy to come to your house and help you with an escape plan.

If there are more than two in the household, and two have escaped safely, one can go for help while the other stays to collect anyone else coming out of the house.

Let the firemen know who isn't out yet and let them go in. That's their job. They are trained and have the equipment to safely negotiate the smoke-filled building. You don't.

Do-It List

- Make a fire escape plan
- Practice fire drills!
- Create a means of escape, if necessary, from upper windows
- Put decals on appropriate windows
- Inspect your fire extinguishers
- Check the batteries on your CO_2 and smoke and/or fire detectors

Chapter 16

First Aid and Emergency Kits

We are not immune to disasters, no matter where we live. If there is one thing the year 2005 taught us it is this: *You have only yourself to count on for help in an emergency.*

Some natural disasters give you fair warning before they hit: hurricanes, thunderstorms—although their attendant tornadoes don't, floods and/or mudslides if there has been too much rain saturating the ground, wildfires in areas of drought, and so on. These you can prepare for ahead of time. You can make evacuation plans in the case of local natural disasters such as hurricanes.

To a certain extent, the disasters you can't predict ahead of time can be prepared for as well.

Create your own emergency preparedness kit, or "go kit" from your own supplies of first aid, food, water, and clothing. Update it as necessary. Some food will have to be replaced if there is an "expiration date" on the product. Water can be replaced if you are filling your own bottles. Clothing should be updated with the seasons.

Just remember, anything can happen in your neighborhood at any time. The wise are prepared.

Beyond Band-Aids®

Basic first aid kits are essential to keep around the house. I once found one of my kids hoarding Band-Aids®! Takes after Mom. Prepared.

Warning
You have to be prepared to help yourself and your family in a natural emergency for *at least* 3 days alone!

Basic First Aid Kit

Here is what the experts have to say. The American Red Cross recommends this collection as the basic first aid kit:

√ Sterile adhesive bandages in assorted sizes—tiny to large

√ Assorted sizes of safety pins

√ Cleansing agent/soap (technical speak for a bottle of hydrogen peroxide and basic soap—no smelly stuff)

√ Latex gloves (2 pairs)

√ Sunscreen (not the whimpy, cute kind either)

√ 2-inch sterile gauze pads (4–6)

√ 4-inch sterile gauze pads (4–6)

√ Triangular bandages (3)

√ Non-prescription drugs

√ 2-inch sterile roller bandages (3 rolls)

√ 3-inch sterile roller bandages (3 rolls)

√ Adhesive tape—the kind you can tear off

√ Scissors

√ Tweezers

√ Needle

√ Moistened towelettes

√ Antiseptic

√ Thermometer

√ Tongue blades (2)

√ Tube (or plastic jar) of petroleum jelly or other lubricant

√ Aspirin or non-aspirin pain reliever

√ Anti-diarrhea medication

√ Antacid (for stomach upset)

√ Syrup of Ipecac (use to induce vomiting if advised by the Poison Control Center)

√ Laxative

√ Activated charcoal (use if advised by the Poison Control Center)

Warning
It usually takes about 3 days for help to arrive and get established into a disaster area. Keep this in mind when packing. Then pack a tad extra (especially in the food department).

Heads UP
Know the weather patterns for where you live and pack reasonably for the seasons you experience.

For the Long Haul—Getting Serious

Face it, the chances of this happening to you are slim at best. But, if it should happen, think earthquake, hurricane, tornado, flood, violent storm, Mother Nature on a rampage, survive it! You will be on your own for awhile. What if you get stranded in your car in a snowstorm? Will you be able to live in the car, or hike out? These are not unreasonable events. Especially in the north.

In winter, you want to pack winter appropriate gear. Likewise in summer. But summer gear doesn't cut it in winter! Those cute hiking sandals are lousy for winter treks.

My friend, Bob Leary, taught survival in the U.S. Army for years, as well as lived it. Here is what he recommends:

Backpack and Fanny pack

Get a sturdy, tough (not bookbag) backpack or rucksack. These can be purchased from Army/Navy surplus stores or catalogs, as well as through sportsman's and outdoor shops. In an emergency, you will be carrying this load yourself and you don't want it falling apart! He has two kits. The really down to basics kit that fits in a fanny pack, and the backpack version. With another set in his vehicle. All these goodies can be found in outdoors and camping shops, hardware stores with camping supply corners, and surplus stores.

In both packs—the minimum

Most of this stuff is quite inexpensive, except the knife—don't get a cheap one! It won't work, nor last.

Knife—Swiss Army-type knife with lots of goodies: sharp blades (serrated is excellent), can openers, tweezers, magnifying glass (start fires with this and a bit of good sunshine), the more goodies the better

Match box and matches/compass/whistle combo—little and versatile (use strike anywhere matches)

Space blanket—the small compact version about the size of the palm of your hand—keeps you warm, very

Prepared Kits

You can purchase kits designed for these situations and already packed.

Either hit the Internet or check with your local Red Cross chapter for more information.

The *Sportsman's Guide* is a catalog of surplus gear sold "cheap" (really). It carries loads of this stuff. It's for hunters as well, so be prepared to look beyond the hunting gear.

warm, if needed (also good to have a spare in the car for keeping your frozen groceries frozen in the summer until you get home)

Poncho—there are the emergency and quite functional kind that are packed to fit in the palm of your hand

Water in canteen—he carries a 2-quart job in his backpack, a smaller one in the fanny pack

Water purification tablets, or the new "straws"

Garbage bags (2)—great quick shelters and ponchos

String saw—this is about a 3' long wire that acts as a saw when you pull it back and forth across tree limbs, great for cutting firewood. Get it at a hardware store.

Energy bars or small food packets

First Aid kit—one of the small compact ones

In addition, in the backpack

Sleeping something, as a lightweight bag. Combine this with a space blanket for more warmth. It crinkles, but hey, it works.

Dehydrated food packs (from the outdoors/camping shops)—lasts forever and they are good food and lightweight

Sturdy boots and/or shoes and a spare pair of socks

Change of clothing, appropriate for the season

Knife—bigger than a pocket knife

Now that you have your kits

Right, you think, what do you do with them?

Keep a kit in your car. Somewhere accessible from the inside in case you get trapped.

In your house, for quick evacuations—place the bag(s) **where you can grab them on the way out.** They may not look cool or fit your decor, but they could save your life.

Ready Made
Check out the various outdoor and "extreme" sports shops as they stock much of this food and safety equipment.

Don't forget your local Army/Navy surplus store.

Prepare Your Own Disaster Survival Kit

Note: The text on this page is in the public domain. It is from "Disaster Supplies Kit" developed by the Federal Emergency Management Agency and the American Red Cross. You can get your own copy from their website, www.redcross.org, as downloadable PDF format or by calling their local chapter phone number.

Review the checklist below. Gather the supplies that are listed. You may need them if your family is confined at home. Place the supplies you'd most likely need for an evacuation in an easy-to-carry container. These supplies are listed with an asterisk (*).

There are six basics you should stock for your home: water, food, first aid supplies, clothing and bedding, tools and emergency supplies, and special items. Keep the items that you would most likely need during an evacuation in an easy-to-carry container—suggested items are marked with an asterisk(*).

Possible Containers Include:
- large, covered trash container
- camping backpack
- duffle bag

Water

Store water in plastic containers such as soft drink bottles. Better yet, outdoors shops have sturdy containers designed for safe water storage, and/or get a water purifying kit. Avoid using containers that will decompose or break, such as milk cartons or glass bottles. A normally active person needs to drink at least two quarts of water each day. Hot environments and intense physical activity can double that amount. Children, nursing mothers, and the ill need more.

Store one gallon of water per person per day. Keep at least a three-day supply of water per person (two quarts for drinking, two quarts for each person in your household for food preparation/sanitation).*

> **Note**
> As they put it so accurately and this is one way to disseminate it, it is offered here verbatim. Some of it has been edited out as it doesn't necessarily apply to you or your situation.

Food

Store at least a **three-day supply** of non-perishable food. Select foods that require no refrigeration, preparation or cooking, and little or no water. If you must heat food, pack a can of Sterno® and a Sterno® stove.

Important
Assemble one kit for your house, one for your car.

You never know when and where you'll need it!

Select food items that are compact and lightweight. *Include a selection of the following foods in your Disaster Supplies Kit:

√ Ready-to-eat canned meats, fruits, and vegetables—dehydrated "camping" foods are terrific, too
√ Canned juices
√ Staples (salt, sugar, pepper, spices, etc.)
√ High energy foods
√ Vitamins
√ Food for infants (if you have one)
√ Comfort/stress foods

Tools and Supplies

√ Mess kits, or paper cups, plates, and plastic utensils*
√ Emergency preparedness manual*
√ Battery-operated radio and extra batteries*
√ Flashlight and extra batteries*
√ Cash or traveler's checks, change*
√ Non-electric can opener, utility knife*
√ Fire extinguisher: small canister ABC type
√ Tube tent
√ Pliers
√ Tape
√ Compass
√ Matches in a waterproof container
√ Aluminum foil
√ Plastic storage containers
√ Signal flare
√ Paper, pencil
√ Needles, thread
√ Medicine dropper

√ Shut-off wrench, to turn off household gas and water
√ Whistle
√ Plastic sheeting
√ Map of the area (for locating shelters)

Sanitation

√ Toilet paper, towelettes*
√ Soap, liquid detergent*
√ Feminine supplies*
√ Personal hygiene items*
√ Plastic garbage bags, ties (for personal sanitation)
√ Plastic bucket with tight lid
√ Disinfectant
√ Household chlorine bleach

Clothing and Bedding

√ Include at least one complete change of clothing and
   footwear per person.*
√ Sturdy shoes or work boots*
√ Rain gear*
√ Blankets or sleeping bags*
√ Hat and gloves
√ Thermal underwear
√ Sunglasses

Special Items

Remember family members with special requirements,
such as infants and elderly or disabled persons

For Adults*

√ Heart and high blood pressure medication
√ Insulin
√ Prescription drugs
√ Denture needs
√ Contact lenses and supplies
√ Extra eye glasses
√ Entertainment
√ Games and books

Have a plan! Make sure you have a way to connect to your family if you get separated. If necessary, make IDs for everyone and make sure everyone carries theirs.

Important Family Documents

ஃ Keep these records in a waterproof, portable container:

√ will, insurance policies, contracts

√ deeds, stocks and bonds

√ passports, social security cards

√ immunization records

√ bank account numbers

√ credit card account numbers and companies

ஃ Inventory of valuable household goods, important telephone numbers

ஃ Family records (birth, marriage, death certificates)

Heed the lessons from 2005's hurricane season—be prepared to help yourself, fight your insurance company, and get yourself back on your own feet.

Store your disaster kit in a convenient place known to all family members. Keep a smaller version of the Disaster Supplies Kit in the trunk of your car.

ஃ Keep items in airtight plastic bags.

ஃ Change your stored water supply every six months so it stays fresh. Replace your stored food every six months.

ஃ Re-think your kit and family needs at least once a year. Replace batteries, update clothes, etc.

ஃ Ask your physician or pharmacist about storing prescription medications.

General Disaster Preparedness Information

"Your Family Disaster Plan" (ARC 4466)

"Your Family Disaster Supplies Kit" (ARC 4463)

This information is available through your local Red Cross office, or via their website: www.redcross.org under Publications, Community Disaster Education Materials.

Visit the FEMA website or office nearest you for plenty of information on preparedness and prevention.

Chapter 17

Suddenly on Your Own

It certainly can happen. Suddenly the power is out, there's a break in the water supply, or something drastic weather-wise interrupts the daily flow of life.

If you are wise, you will have made some preparations for at least the most predictable of these events. Watch the weather forecasts with an eye to problem storms or situations that may affect you. If you see a huge storm coming, fill a couple of gallon containers with fresh water, get out the candles and matches. Some of this information is obvious. Some may not be.

Even smarter, get a NOAA weather radio—one with a battery backup. In the event of a coming disaster, the radio will blast out a warning in the case of tornadoes and such, or keep you posted on coming scary weather. That is—as long as it is always kept on. For any of you living in areas constantly hit with sudden storms or drastic weather events, you can't be without one of these.

Alerts

If your cell phone can receive weather alerts, and you live in an area prone to violent weather, set up your phone to receive alerts.

Extra provisions

Always, but always, have canned food hanging around. Rotate it to use up the older food first. Have at least a week's worth and a variety of items—stuff that you really like to eat, ad nauseam. Because you just may be eating it ad nauseam. One of our staples is baked beans. They are easy to cook and don't taste bad cold.

Or go to a camping/outdoors or surplus store, and stock up on MRE Army surplus (Meals Ready to Eat) or the dehydrated camping food in foil packets. All you add is water. Which of course, you have to stock, too.

Things to have on hand

√ Sterno® stove (collapsible) and plenty of Sterno® fuel pots—this is for cooking your canned food

√ Candles, the long lasting type

√ Oil lamps and plenty of lamp oil

√ Flashlights and plenty of batteries

√ Matches, the safety and non-safety types (if you have children or are prone to dropping stuff, use the safety version)

√ Containers (clean milk gallon jugs work very well) for water—with lids

√ Paper plates and bowls, plastic utensils—you may not get a chance to wash anything

√ Water purifying tablets

√ Extra blankets or comforters if it is cold

√ Moist towelettes for cleaning your hands, too

√ Radio: battery-powered, or solar/hand-crank type, sold through surplus stores as well as radio shops

In case of Loss of Water

If it's just your house, get a plumber or the septic pro quickly—and ask your nice neighbor if you can use their facilities. That's obvious.

But what if you are dumped on in a huge snow storm with no power, and therefore no water, no help, no nothing! You have a problem. Again, in snow country, many of us have wood stoves as backup for heat and cooking. If you don't have one, and your area is prone to long blackouts, installing a woodstove and chimney is a good idea.

If you see this situation coming your way, via the weather reports, don't hesitate to fill the bathtub with some water.

Heads Up

You may think of more items that are important to you to have on hand in an emergency.

Keep a list of possibilities as you think of them, then get the items and store them in an easy-to-reach place.

You can use the water to flush the toilets (if you have your own well system—as these are run by electric pumps), or, when boiled, to cook with. If the storm passes and you don't have a problem, don't just run the water out, water your grateful plants.

In case of a Power Outage

First of all, you had better store those candles and oil lamps in easily accessible places—where you can find them in an emergency without stumbling over chairs in the dark.

Keep the oil lamps clean and filled. Understand that the wicks will evaporate the oil over time, so you want to check them periodically as well as clean the lamp chimneys. If you keep flashlights around (with fresh batteries) you can easily use the flashlights to find the oil lamps.

An even smarter trick is to have one nightlight that is also an emergency flashlight. It plugs in as usual, but when the power goes out, it comes on as a flashlight. Get them at hardware stores. Put it someplace where light is useful when the power goes out—say a central hallway or the living room. Ours is good for 90 minutes without a recharge. It has come in handy quite a few times.

If you have a wood-burning stove or fireplace, make sure there is always wood in a safe and dry place for use in an emergency. If you use wood often, make sure your put-to-the-side emergency wood pile hasn't turned punk in the meantime. Hardware stores sell packed paraffin and wood-chip logs that would be a good choice (as they remain dry) to store for emergencies.

If you use kerosene heaters, make sure the rooms are ventilated properly or you will kill yourself with the fumes and gases. Follow the manufacturer's directions to the letter!

In case of a Natural Disaster

If you get hit with a natural disaster you will be directed by the proper authorities to the assigned shelter for your area. You don't have much choice in the matter, unless

Right
Don't think it can happen to you? Suppose a car crashes into a nearby electric pole, or a transformer blows, or you are simply scheduled for blackouts!

Have Fun!
Keep a deck of cards, books, or board games handy to entertain you when it's dark. Beats staring into the dark.

you have made previous arrangements to go elsewhere—hopefully before the disaster hits—and/or you can get there on your own.

It's an excellent idea to have a backup place to go and stay. Willing relatives, close friends, people who you don't mind offering the same in exchange should they be displaced by a disaster.

Post Katrina
Plan a rendezvous place, either via phone, email, or in person where everyone can check-in with everyone else. That way, searches can be started for anyone missing.

Make arrangements to have a contact outside of your area with whom family members can connect to notify them of their whereabouts. After Hurricane Katrina, too many families were separated by rescuers, and circumstances, losing contact with each other—literally.

If a family member is incapable of speaking for him- or herself, make an ID for that person to carry or wear. Especially small children and for the elderly. If someone has health problems and needs special care, indicate that. Add your special outside contact number to the ID as well.

If you have pets

Don't forget to make arrangements for your defenseless pets, should you have some. Shelters may not take pets. It would be a good idea to check with the local authorities—before an emergency—to see what, if any, provisions are made for Fluffy and Fido.

Chapter 18

Beyond the Deadbolt

Depending on where you live, you may or may not need serious extra precautions with security. If security is a big issue in your neighborhood, don't hesitate to call in an expert security company immediately. Have them look over your situation and evaluate it.

If you contacted your local police when you first moved in, as suggested earlier, then you should have a pretty good idea of your situation.

Be reasonable about this. You can live as if your neighborhood is an armed camp—even when it isn't. In other neighborhoods, that attitude may be the norm. It's up to you to know what works where you live.

Cheap? Sometimes, the act of just putting security company stickers on your doors is enough to keep the bad guys at bay.

But, don't count on it.

Beyond the Deadbolt

Wood/steel doors

Use deadbolt locks, in addition to your regular door lock, with a bolt that goes at least one inch into the door frame and structural framing behind it—so the door can't be kicked open. If you don't have one already installed, have a locksmith install one for you—on all your outside doors. Make sure you have enough spare keys to give to family members, or a neighbor you trust in case of an emergency, in addition to one easily reached in an emergency such as a quick escape from a fire. You don't want to lock yourself in when you desperately need to get out either.

Glass doors

For those sliding patio doors, cut an old broom stick just a bit shorter than the exposed channel where the door slides, and drop the wood down in the groove. That will keep the door from opening if someone tries to break in.

Window locks

Make sure that all your windows have strong locking mechanisms on them. You can do for sliding windows what you did for a sliding door. You can also put a length of pole in the top of double-hung windows, along the sides. You may want to figure out a way to prevent them from being wiggled out by an enterprising burglar—a bit of Velcro® to stick the pole in place.

Lighting

Have decent lighting around your house. It's hard for the bad guys to find refuge in bright light.

Consider using timers for lights and radios so you don't come home to a dark and quiet house. Timers are available at hardware stores in the electrical aisles.

Landscaping

As much as you love to squish plants and bushes up against your house, you want to make sure they don't offer the ultimate hiding place for bad guys. Trim them down to unusable hiding-place size. If you love those bushes but they are too easy to use against you, move them and replace them with some growing lovely that doesn't offer easy hiding quarters.

While on vacation

It is a good idea to let a trusted neighbor or two know your plans and ask them to keep an eye on your house for you. If they can, have them pick up any packages dropped at your door, and retrieve your mail.

If you have a security system in your home, notify the company of your plans, and where to find you.

Window Stop

If you want to open your window a little bit for air, but want protection: Drill a small hole the size of a 10p nail (big "common" nail—the one with a head on it) through the window frames and stick a nail in it. The nail will help prevent someone from outside opening the window.

What to leave on, what to shut off

If you want to save money, as well as potentially all your electronic stuff from power surges or lightning strikes while on your vacation, unplug all electronic goodies that you won't use while you are away: televisions, CD players, radios, computers, printers, microwave, VCR, cable boxes—anything that can get zapped by lightning that doesn't need to be plugged in while you aren't there. Not only are you protecting them in case of a bad storm, you are saving money.

Turn off your electric water heater at the circuit breaker. You won't be needing the water while you are gone and it doesn't take that long to warm up the tank again when you return. If you look forward to a hot tub when you return, perhaps your trusted neighbor will turn it on for you just before your arrival.

If you have a gas water heater, you can turn down the temperature while you are gone. Check the unit for a "vacation" setting and turn the knob, then jack it up upon your return. Saves gas.

Turn off the water to the washing machine. There should be a mixing valve switch where the lines join hot and cold from the washer to the house supply.

Again, get some timers for the radio and some of your lights—the bedroom and living room for starters and set them to run about the times you are home.

If you have a spare car, leave it where it can be seen in the driveway. Or have someone else park their vehicle in your driveway and use it.

For a summer vacation:

If you have an air-conditioner, turn it a bit higher, or have it cycle on for only a few hours a day if the temperatures will be humid. If you don't live in a humid environment, just turn it off.

Lower the shades on the south and west-facing windows to keep the heat out and the temperature down.

Warning
Anything you do to windows, remember, you may need to get out of them in an emergency.

Stop deliveries

√ Don't forget to stop any newspaper or food deliveries to the house.

√ Make arrangements for any other deliveries, say UPS or FedEx, to be dropped off at a neighbor's house.

√ Ask your postal office to hold your mail until your return, or have a neighbor pick it up for you every day. You can return the favor when they go on vacation.

Vacation Check-Off List

❧ Stop newspaper delivery

❧ Have mail held or dealt with

❧ Deal with the water heater

❧ Unplug the electrical stuff

Part V

Community— Becoming a Neighbor

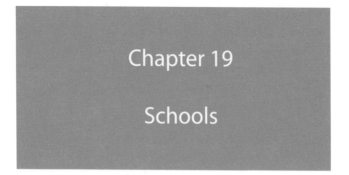

Chapter 19

Schools

Nothing can make or break a community like schools. A good school can be the centerpiece of activities. A bad school is a thorn in everyone's side.

Good schools have plenty of parental input. Parents help out as aides, with fundraising for special projects, teaching computers, planning, whatever is needed.

> When my children were in elementary school, I taught computers to the early grades (in the early 1980s), and we parents helped with the after-school sports programs. Parents put on parties at Halloween and Christmas. That school was ranked as one of the best elementary schools in the entire country. And we parents had a lot to do with it.

Bad schools destroy. They hurt the children, the community, the spirit of everyone. They are the source of much acrimony. But there is one way to change that. Get involved. If you have children in school—get involved now. If you will have children who will go to the schools eventually, get involved now. Hopefully, you can change matters before your children are stuck in a bad situation.

Volunteer

If you have an expertise that can be easily shared with children, offer to hold an after-school program. My

Fact
Your child only gets one opportunity at an excellent education. Our future depends on it.

Schools

children learned chess in such a program. Before we had regular foreign language instruction, we had a French teacher offer his services to the kids. I've given writing workshops at several schools, as part of regular classes as well as after-school workshops.

Know your child

Be realistic about your child's strengths and weaknesses. You must know your child and be ready to fight for his or her future. It may not be in your child's best interests to have the school's administration tell you what's best. Evaluate the schools on the basis of your child's strengths.

Is there a choice?

Parental concern for the worsening educational system has "reached critical mass," according to the Center for Education Reform. Concerned parents, educators and politicians, tired of lowered standards for educational content, lowered test scores and unhappy, under-educated children, are finally doing something about the situation.

If the reforms haven't come to your state and you want them, contact your local representative and start doing something about it. The "something" is school choice.

Normally, your child is assigned to a public school. You don't have a choice. Or rather, didn't. Increasingly that is changing.

According to Education Week and Teacher Magazine website (www.edweek.org) there are five types of school choice: Intradistrict choice, Controlled choice, Magnet schools, Charter schools, and Voucher plans.

Another source of information is The Center for Education Reform. As the laws keep changing, it is worth visiting their website to keep up to date on the subject if this is of interest. (www.edreform.com)

If you have Internet access, visit www.theschoolreport. com, a site where you can compare all the schools in

Speak Up
If there are school board meetings open to the public, attend them. If there are matters to vote on, do so. But only if you understand what is being voted on.

your area. It also has plenty of other information that can be helpful.

If there is a choice, make it wisely. It will be up to you to shop around as you would for any other commodity. Remember to keep your child's interests in mind as a priority. If a school is athletically oriented and your child is more scholarly, look elsewhere.

Public schools

Public schools are just that, funded by public taxes, states and the federal government. The community's children are expected to attend. Parents are asked to participate, at least in the voting of budgets, maybe chaperoning parties, and perhaps fundraisers. They usually have some sort of Parents and Teachers Organization or Association (PTO or PTA) as a way to get parents to participate in the school.

For the elementary school level:

At the suggestion of an elementary school principal, visit the school, visit the classrooms, and watch the children.

√ Are they happy, lively, and chatty?

√ Do they look and act challenged?

√ Do they want to answer the questions put to them?

√ Do they play together well?

√ Is the school bright? Full of children's art work and efforts?

√ Is the school active with computers, or perhaps a sister school to some other distant school?

Visit Before enrolling your child(ren), spend time at the school. Speak with teachers, students, the administration and others involved with the school. You can get a pretty good feel for the school that way.

For example, our local school and its principal were the co-founders of Project Harmony which started to connect American children with children and teachers in Russia during the communist era. My daughter had a painting sent over to be displayed in a Russian school in an exchange of art work. Their teachers came here, and our teachers went there to teach and learn. It was an eye-opening experience for all involved.

High school students

Consider these issues especially when choosing a high school for your children:

√ Do they have active arts programs? Do they put on plays, musicals, concerts? Is the public invited to these events?

√ What is their athletic program like? Are only the choice athletes chosen? Or can any child participate? Is there a variety of sports programs or do they concentrate on just the big sports, i.e., football, soccer, baseball, and basketball?

√ Is there a serious clique problem at school, where the unchosen students are snubbed, ignored, or worse? Where would your child fit in?

√ How does the school deal with gifted students? Are there programs for them? Or are they left in regular classes, bored to tears. Are the Honors classes really advanced? Or in name only.

√ What is their special education policy? How are those students treated? To fill classes dumbed down (meaning lowered standards such as making a one-year course a two-year course), does the administration put in children who deserve more?

Dumbing down

Does the school "dumb" down the classwork, or challenge the students?

For example, one high school split Algebra I into two years, one year for each normal semester, thinking the students "weren't ready for Algebra I." The course was dumbed down instead of challenging students to excel. Students who could have taken four years of advanced math didn't get enough math courses for college and hurt their chances for college admission. Because of this dumbing down policy, the Vermont state colleges have had to hold remedial math classes to bring students current for more serious courses, adding another year at college. And of course, more expenses for the student and parents.

√ What about drugs on campus? What is the school's policy? Do they work with the police on this issue, or prefer to deal with it themselves? If you have any doubt, walk into a school bathroom and sniff. Watch the students. Do they look alert? Or zoned out?

√ Hang around the classes. Is there fighting or learning going on? Is the teacher in control? Or are the students fractious?

√ Is there smoking on campus? Not allowed, or only in a special place? Preferably, not allowed at all.

√ How does the administration deal with you and your child when you go in for a meeting? Are you comfortable? More importantly, how does your child feel at these meetings? Trust your child's instincts. How does the administration deal with the students?

If you are unhappy with your local public schools, look elsewhere. Keep in mind that private and other non-public schools probably don't offer bus transportation to and from the school. That will be your responsibility.

As with any major decision, do your homework. If you choose to attend other than a public school, check with the State Education department, other students who attend that school, and most importantly, the teachers' credentials.

Charter schools

Many states allow charter schools. Because of the lack of restrictions and red tape, charter schools are free to concentrate on what the students need to excel as opposed to what the Feds tell them to do. As they are consumer-driven, rather than mandated to act a certain way, charter schools are increasingly popular. If the school doesn't produce well-educated students, the school will be forced to close. As they are designed for specific strengths whether it be science, sports, or arts; they attract excellent teachers and supporters. If your child is more interested in a charter school's curriculum than that offered in the public school, then seriously consider sending your child to the charter school.

Charter Schools

A charter school is an independent public school, free of the restrictions placed on the standard public schools.

There is a caveat to charter schools. They are allowed to take only the students they want. If your child doesn't fit their mold, or the school doesn't want him or her—you are out of luck. Also, they are not required to take Special Ed students. Charter schools drain funds away from regular schools—and the students still attending them. This could be your child. Special Education budgets are fixed on a per student basis. If your local school loses students to charter schools, then those lost funds come from the budget for the regular student body. It doesn't affect the special education budget. That's why so many of the programs at the public schools get cut.

Private schools

Private schools are just that, private. You pay the tuition, your child must gain entrance. The same criteria for choosing public schools holds here as well. Some schools are better than others for sports, academics, the arts, or other special programs. If your child has an interest or talent far beyond what is offered at your local school, look for a private school. Scholarships and tuition help may be available, depending on your financial circumstances.

Each child is special

There are children who just can't thrive in a public school, but excel in a private one geared to their abilities and talents.

If your child needs the benefits of a private school, look for the right one. If the school isn't close to you, your child will have to board there. If you are very lucky, there will be a good school within driving distance.

To find a private school, ask friends whose children attend one, or ask a guidance counselor at a public school, ask your local librarian, surf the web, check out the classifieds in *New York Times Sunday Magazine* among others.

Another information source is About.com's website (see Resources). It will lead you to a vast source of information including financial aid sites. Another site is ISACS, or the Independent Schools Associations of the Central States. The NEASC or New England Association of Schools and Colleges is another source of private school information.

Religious schools

These are private schools with a religious philosophy, whether it be traditional Catholic schools run by nuns, to the Christian schools of today. If you don't want your child steeped in religion, don't consider them. If you prefer a religious background, do look into them. Make sure that their curriculum is state approved and that the children are learning the basics along with the religion. Your church will know where to find the schools.

Get Program of Studies

In looking at any school, get a Program of Studies, a list of all the classes offered by the school. This is particularly important for seventh grade and up when students start directing their interests into what they may choose as their ultimate career. Check the program carefully.

If your child is interested in a technical career, is that option available? Not every child is destined for an ivy-league college. But, if your child is interested in college, are the classes there?

Suppose your child is interested in sciences. Look into the classrooms and ask the school:

√ What is the science department like?

√ Do they have excellent labs or out-dated equipment?

√ Are the teachers interested in their subject, or are they there to fill time until they can collect their pension?

√ Is the class a challenge? Or routine?

√ Can your child get into the classes with the best teachers?

√ Do the students have a chance at science fairs?

√ Much of this information can be gleaned from actually visiting a class in progress. Observe the students at work. Are they involved or chatting on the side? Is this a hands on class? Or endless lectures?

Program of Studies
Work out a program with your child for the years he or she will be attending school. Make sure the classes are available when your child can take the courses.

Sports programs

Most schools have a sports program of some sort. Whether it be the lifeblood of the school's pride and esteem or simply out for fun. Granted an excellent team can put the school on the map. But at what expense? Are the team members good students too? Or are they promoted or handled for their on-field prowess only?

What sports does the school promote? How much budget goes into the sports programs as opposed to the other school functions?

Heads UP
Are the students actually getting into the classes they need to graduate? How available are they?

If your child is athletically inclined, is he or she a team player or more individual? Therefore, does the school promote track and field, cross-country running, biking, football, baseball, basketball, tennis, skiing (in the north), or soccer? How hard is it to get on a team? What are the coaches like?

For that matter, what are the physical education teachers like? Are they fit? Can they do what they ask the students to do? Don't laugh, I know of a high school with two obese gym teachers who drove to the playing fields across the road. But these teachers had tenure and couldn't be fired or removed without a great deal of expense.

Meet with the guidance office or admin

Now that you have this bundle of questions tucked in your head, it's time to make an appointment with the Guidance Office and/or the Administration.

Armed with your child's proposed schedule, can your child get into the chosen classes?

How accommodating is the schedule or the guidance counselor? If you don't like this particular counselor (and that happens), is another counselor open for new students?

Find out how many credits your child needs to graduate from high school. How long does it take to get these credits?

If a student only needs 20 credits to graduate, can these credits be done in only three years instead of four? Or is there only one credit left to take in the senior year that could have been taken in the junior year to graduate early?

Do some of the Industrial Arts classes qualify as math classes and therefore your child doesn't need higher math? If your child is college-bound, make sure they get into the higher math classes anyway.

If you are happy and your student is happy, it's time to register. If you are not happy, start looking elsewhere.

Registering your children

When you register your student, you will need to have a copy to give, or be able to have a copy of the earlier school transcripts sent to the new school. The transcripts are a record of your child's course schedules, grades and perhaps other academic achievements already completed.

In most states, you will need a record of your child's immunization records from birth. If you don't have them handy, can you get them from your previous health care providers? If you intentionally didn't have your child immunized, then find out what you need to do to register your child without having to go through the immunization process.

If your child is on medications or has allergies or special needs, the school must be advised. There is a policy to handle all these needs. In the case of medications, school nurses will be required to administer the medications.

Have a list of names, addresses, and in particular, phone numbers where you, your spouse, or someone else who knows your child well or can be trusted by you and your child, can be reached in an emergency. Also, the names and phone numbers of medical and dental providers.

Try to get a floor plan of the school and walk with your child through the school to their classes. Or if the child is old enough, he or she may want to do this alone. How long is the bell between classes? Is there enough time for

So...visit! Don't hesitate to visit a prospective school. Check out the security arrangements and other safety issues.

Pick up plan Have a plan worked out with your child in case of an emergency. There have been a lot of nasty events happening in schools lately. Have a plan to contact your child and/or pick them up.

the student to get from one class to another? As schools try to push the class schedules to excess, there may only be three minutes to run from one end of the school to the other. Any advance practice on the student's part is a bonus.

How do the kids get there?

If you live within blocks of the schools, getting there isn't much of an issue. Walking is healthy. Don't bother with this section.

However, if you aren't that close to the school, getting there is usually by bus. Provided a route is near your house, and the bus isn't full.

In the suburbs, the children usually troop over to a designated spot by a specific time and the bus shows up to collect the children and deliver them safely to school. In more rural areas, the driver collects children at the bottom of your driveway or street.

At least in theory.

Sometimes there are too many children for a route, sometimes the drivers aren't perfect and run late, or don't show up. Or a bus breaks down before collecting the children.

Be prepared for any contingency. If you can see your children waiting for the bus from your house, all the better. You can keep an eye out for them. Or if they are younger children, wait with them.

If you can't see them and they are with a group of children, is someone available to watch or be with the kids? There can be serious issues among children if there are older children who wish to dominate the younger ones and bully them.

Especially in northern climes, if the temperature is brutally cold, *don't allow the children to wait long for a bus*. If the bus is late, the children aren't dressed properly, or something goes wrong, your child could suffer serious frostbite or worse. It has happened.

Listen to your child

Does your child like the counselor? If not, ask for another. Please! If your child and the counselor don't like each other, you will never hear the end of it. And your child may suffer as a result.

Bus Information:

√ While at the school, find out the bus schedule and routes.

√ What bus will your child take?

√ What is the number of the bus?

√ When is it due at your stop?

How does the administration handle late buses or those that don't show up (due to breakdown or something)? Are the kids punished for being late or absent? Or is the administration helpful about the situation? Will the teachers allow some latitude with homework and other assignments in such a situation?

Get to know the driver, if possible. Be there with your child when the bus first comes and introduce yourself and your child. Don't be shy about it.

Younger children should know their driver to be confident that they are on the right bus and will get home to mom or dad safely.

Check to see if the buses have safety belts on them and that the children use them. If they don't have belts, why not? While many school districts have the belts installed, the children aren't required to use them unless they are on a field trip going some distance from the school.

Know the laws about passing school buses. The law is quite simple. Don't do it while the bus is discharging children. The bus will have flashing red lights while the kids are actually leaving the bus and crossing the streets. If you do try to pass a bus, the driver will most assuredly get your license and report you. The fines are hefty. Those are your children's and your neighbors children's lives at stake.

For older children with a driver's license, what are the rules for driving to school and parking? It is common for seniors with licenses to drive to school. (They don't want to be caught dead on a bus!) They will need to register their car with the school, prove they have the proper insurance for the car, and obtain a parking permit and perhaps their own assigned space.

> **Warning**
> Don't discount the possible threat of someone trying to "pick up" your child "to take them to school." Make sure your child(ren) know whom to allow to pick them up and whom to avoid.

> Some schools may not have enough parking for the seniors as well as the staff and may only allow children with jobs after school to apply for parking and driving permission.

Get involved with the PTO/PTA

Parent Teacher Organization (PTO) and Parent Teacher Association (PTA) are the link between parents, faculty, and the administration within a school.

PTA

PTA is a national organization that lobbies and advocates on behalf of children in Washington. They charge membership fees and hold regular meetings throughout the year. It is a very organized institution. If you want to know more, try their website at www.pta.org, or ask at your school.

PTO

PTOs, on the other hand, are a locally organized group of parents doing their volunteering for that particular school. Our PTO organizes the Halloween party, the huge fall fundraiser for the children's after-school sports activities; they bought the first computers for the school in the 1980s. They do whatever the group will organize itself to do.

These organizations can be an invaluable resource for any school. Working with the administration, they can fill in the gaps in funding, bringing in special arts programs, organizing and funding field trips, craft bazaars, Christmas parties and whatever else is needed, but not necessarily provided or budgeted by the school.

Home schooling

This is increasingly an option if you prefer to teach your children yourself. As of 1999, there were about 1.2 million children being homeschooled, according to experts, or about 2% of the school population, with that number growing more every year.

If you choose to homeschool your children, call your State's Education department (found in the white pages) and ask

Join!
Once your child is registered and attending school, ask about the PTO or PTA and join the group. It's a great way to meet other parents and become active in your community.

if they have any special requirements that must be met for your child to "graduate" or at least qualify as a graduate. Vermont has a listing for Home & Independent Schools under State of Vermont, Education, so look under your own state's listings for Education to see if they have a specific number to call. If not, call the main Education number.

Your child will have to be "enrolled" with your state as a student in a homeschool. The state will want the names, addresses, ages and other information about your child before enrolling.

For an example of what is required by the state to home-school, in Vermont you will have to arrange a yearly assessment of your child's progress in each subject by one or more of the following:

1) a certified teacher,

2) a teacher from an approved Vermont school,

3) a commercial curriculum publisher's teacher advisory service report along with a portfolio of your child's work,

4) standardized achievement test results (administered by a qualified person or by an approved Vermont school),

5) "a report prepared by the parents or the student's instructor together with a portfolio of the student's work."

Resources for home schooling

If you have a computer with Internet access, visit the websites listed in Resources. They are loaded with information and links to even more sites that are appropriate.

Another site, run by *Home Education Magazine*, itself a valuable resource, with links to each state's website with the requirements for homeschooling legally.

If you don't yet have a computer with Internet access and plan to homeschool, get one. There are many invaluable tools for both you and your children online from books,

Connected

With the availability of the Internet, it is easier than ever to homeschool as there is endless information available at your fingertips.

newsletters, support groups, to college courses through universities.

One issue that may worry parents is the lack of contact with other children the same ages as yours. If your student wishes to participate in the local school's activities as well as homeschool, check with the local public school itself.

Many schools are willing to have homeschoolers join a class, use their playgrounds, or be part of a team. You can work with your local schools and in fact, may have to, to have your child's work be accredited for advancement and graduation.

Chapter 20

Part of a Community

Day care, playgroups, baseball diamonds, soccer teams, parks to walk in, places the kids can play. This information should be available from your real estate agent and you can learn much from just driving around. However, asking neighbors, making a few phone calls, asking at the schools are also ways to join in the recreational activities.

Find the local bulletin boards posted in supermarkets, post offices, banks, and other locations to see what is happening in your neighborhood. From local theater productions, to offerings to start a playgroup, to dance and music lessons, tutoring, cars for sale, the bulletin board is the local news board.

Get the local paper

Maybe it's only a weekly paper, or an occasional offering, but if there is a newspaper for your community, do sub-scribe. That paper is the reflection of the lifeblood of your community.

This is a great way to get a feel for your new community. As well as a great way to find out how to get involved. You will see the same names over and over. When you "run into" one of these people, introduce yourself and tell him or her that you are a newcomer.

There will be a section devoted to current events and happenings. Pick an event that interests you and go.

Events
Stay current on area events. If the event is open to the public, by all means go and support it.

Sign up at the Library

Libraries are a terrific way to get information about a place. Most have children's events, readings, and story-tellings, making them a perfect place to find new friends for your young children.

Many sponsor book clubs and readings. Often, a local citizen will offer to hold a workshop or slide show. These are quite popular where I live. It makes for a great social hour. Especially during the winter.

Offer your services for an hour or so once a week or month. Sorting and stamping books isn't a great rush, but it is a help. It's a great way to get to know your neighbors and find others interested in the same things you are. That way you meet people you otherwise may have missed. Join the reading group. There you'll meet people with the same interests, at least in literature.

If you have small children, offer to hold a children's story hour if it isn't done. Another way to exchange time and play periods with fellow mothers and playmates.

At the very least, you'll have access to loads of books—and bump into potential new friends.

Take a class

Ten years ago, I took a watercolor class and met a new fellow in town. As we spoke to each other we discovered that we were both writers, as is his wife; they both loved and enjoyed working in the theater and they had just moved to the area a month before. They have been my closest friends ever since. I conned them into joining our local theater group, as well as our statewide writers group where we were on the Board of Directors together. If I hadn't taken that class, we may very well have missed each other.

Find Activities

Check your local phone book. Many list facilities and how to find them or get there. In Vermont, not only are local facilities listed, but state ones as well, including state parks, bike and hiking trails, public pools, museums, and libraries among other adventures.

Take a walk, go hiking, go biking

There's bound to be a community path, park, or playground, or something of the sort. Use it. While on a group bike ride I met a woman whose path I never would have crossed otherwise. As we crashed our way through the woods together, we talked about what we did. I wrote books, she designed them; another friend with common interests.

After the first edition of this book was written, a friend asked what she should do when walking in the woods, as she was a bit worried about bears. I suggested she "take a dog along and talk to it!" She got herself a puppy for her walks. Last I heard, she was thrilled.

Join the theater!

You never know if you'll be the next local star. Even if you can't act, working backstage, on props, or helping with publicity is a great opening into the community. Attend a show and if you enjoyed it, hang around until the actors and crew start milling around (they always do), or go backstage and start talking to them. Offer your services for the next production. Don't be shy about it.

Local theater has got to be one of the surest ways to meet interesting people, get seriously involved in fun, and keep yourself busy. Not to mention a new network of friends, and possible business contacts. Especially if you are self-employed.

Of course, if you wish to cavort onstage, by all means do so. Tryouts and auditions are announced in local papers usually well ahead of time. Show up and go for it! Offer your services either way. Even musicals have parts for non-singers—and non-dancers.

You don't have to make a complete fool of yourself on stage to be a part of a theater group. There are plenty of backstage jobs to be done. And usually, there are more

Fame?

I kept getting typecast as a bimbo... I can't imagine what they were thinking.... When I outgrew the bimbo roles I started running lights for productions. I'm still having fun!

people backstage than onstage. Even the shy can fit comfortably in such a group.

Some of the offstage jobs needed to run a theater are:

Drat!

One "unfortunate" side-effect is the possible weight gain from all those cast parties!

- ♠ director and assistant director
- ♠ producer
- ♠ musical director (for musicals)
- ♠ stage manager and stage hands
- ♠ costumes, makeup, and props
- ♠ lighting and lighting design
- ♠ set design and construction
- ♠ media and advertising (designing posters and selling ads for the playbill)

Naturally, the bigger the play or musical, the bigger the crew to run the event. Usually, local theaters are open, friendly, non-professional, and very willing to accept any offer of help. Especially from newcomers. Talent of any kind is welcome and quickly put to use. There is a burn-out factor when only a small core of people put on show after show. If there are lots of people involved, the load is shared and more fun.

Joining is easy, ask neighbors and friends if they know anything; go to a show, hang around afterwards and talk with someone in the show; pop in on a rehearsal; check the local papers for meetings, auditions, and rehearsal schedules and drop in.

Membership "fees" are usually paltry. Our membership fee is free if you work on shows, and then $5 and up depending on how much you wish to contribute. As most local theater groups are non-profit, membership fees are used to run the theater and put on shows.

Church organizations

There's bound to be a church in your new community. If it works for you, join it. Try a lot of churches! Many are variations on various themes of religion, yet similar in other ways. The closest church may be perfect, or it may not.

Look around until you find one you are comfortable with. Offer to help with church activities. Offer your talents.

Join their choir, the women's groups, a lay group. Get involved. Don't try to take over and lead before you know what's going on. Not a good idea.

School groups

If you have children in school, by all means offer your services and talents to the school and the students. I've taken a day off to teach writing at our local high school and other middle schools. It's quite a trip. When my kids were little, I taught computers to the elementary students. It's a great way to meet your children's friend's parents—or other parents with children yours might enjoy that they would not have met otherwise.

Chambers of Commerce

If you are a home-business person—join the Chamber. It will aid your business' visibility and introduce you around—for free. If you have a business that can do a service to help, say, typesetting—offer your services. Even if your name isn't splattered all over the job, your good deed will get noticed.

Besides, you'll meet a lot of like-minded souls.

Volunteering

This is one of the best ways to get involved in a community. Read the local paper and see what's going on around you. If you see where help is needed, jump in and offer your services. If a neighbor needs help and you can't do it alone, find a bunch of people who can.

Join Activities! Try joining: local theater, library groups, take a class, take a hike! If you take a friendly dog for a walk, you are sure to meet people.

Years ago, one of our beloved neighbors, Henry, then 92, was declared legally blind. Out of the woodwork, literally, came a legion of his friends and volunteers to spend time with him, drive him on his errands, check in on him, be with him when necessary, cook for him, and generally take care of him so he could live on his own. One was his mentor until Henry's death, organizing everything "Henry." Two of us tapped his friends for $5 each to start an emergency phone system so that when he was alone, he was able to push a button and call for help. We received so much money that we started an emergency phone system for all the seniors in our community. The commercial emergency systems available at that time were too expensive for our seniors to indulge in. Within days of our announcement, an answering service called us and offered to create and monitor such a system. For the sum of $5/month—*if the client had the money*, we offered a "panic" button to use in emergencies. If the client didn't have the money, our fundraiser had already paid for it anyway— the client still had the button. That system lasted for 18 years until it wasn't needed as the state started offering the same service as part of the Home Health Service.

The Rural Life

Moving to the country from the city is the equivalent of moving to foreign country for most people. Just about everything is different, starting with how fast, or rather, how much slower and more casual life is.

How you are accepted into the community depends entirely on how you behave. You will be treated as you treat others. If you are friendly and open you will be welcomed as such. If you treat the locals like idiots, you will be treated like an idiot. Don't assume that just because you're from the big city you "know more." You don't.

You just know different things. Besides, that local you snubbed as an idiot just may be a retired molecular physicist. If you think this isn't an issue, I've been on the receiving end of some "flatlanders" who thought they knew better. Let me tell you, I grew up in Washington, DC, lived in London, Germany, and The Netherlands before moving to the country. I've been here over 30 years and wouldn't live anywhere else.

Warning
Please don't take your fast-paced lifestyle with you into the country and expect everyone already there to adjust to you.

It works the other way.

You must readjust yourself to your new community.

Driving

You may notice that people wave to one another when driving by a friend. They drive less frenetically, although maybe just as fast. They don't honk when unhappy, they are willing to wait. You may have to deal with farm wagons and tractors during planting and harvesting seasons. Those things are slow, but they are part of what makes your new community what it is—country. If you are patient, the farmer will pull over to let you by when it is safe to do so. Watch for his hand signals. Or he may be traveling just a few fields and will be getting off the road quickly anyway. Don't try to pass a tractor without really checking carefully. That tractor may be turning left just as you accelerate.

Dress up?

In the country? Who ever heard of such a thing? Dressing up in the country can be just wearing a clean shirt and pants. A visit to the bank manager isn't an ordeal, but a quick drop-in. Although, the bank manager may have on a better set of overalls (just kidding, our bank employees are "dressed up" in more business-like attire). The last time I wore high heels was on stage! Put away your serious business and dress-up clothing and relax. Dress for the weather. If it is cold, dress properly. Couture doesn't count, sensible does.

Local Hangouts

The food store, post office, recycling center, and dump are the big hang-outs. That's where you run into everyone you know at one time or another. Getting around the store for just one item may take you an hour. Just too many friends to visit!

Secrets, what secrets?

Get used to the fact that everyone knows just about everything about each other. It's downright hard to keep a secret. If you are famous, and you become one of the community, you'll find that your new friends won't let on to strangers that you even exist.

> **Dents**
> You can make a difference where you live. Take the opportunity to make the most of it.

If a stranger shows up on your doorstep with a bundle, it's probably a welcoming neighbor bringing something edible over. Invite your new friend in and offer something to drink (try tea or coffee, first).

If you have a talent, offer your services. Our schools have been the lucky recipients of after-school chess clubs; jazz musicians teaching and leading bands; dancers, writers, and actors leading workshops; storytellings; and numerous other gifts of time.

When a catastrophe occurs, within minutes there are neighbors to help. The letters to the editor of our local paper attest to the newcomers astounded at the selflessness of the community in times of crisis. If you can help, offer to! Rural residents are very self-sufficient. They have to be to survive.

> "Go knock on a neighbor's door with an apple pie. And if you can't bake one, then buy one, cook it and take it anyway. Works every time!"
>
> Bob Leary, US Army, Retired

Join the ambulance service

They offer free training to anyone who wants to help with rescue efforts. If you aren't up to dealing with the accidents, pain, and suffering, you could help with the dispatch work. Even one day a week is a help as most of the programs are volunteers only.

Help with the senior citizens meals programs. Or be a visitor, checking on the seniors to make sure they are healthy.

Join the Fire Department

Volunteer fire departments are always looking for help. You don't have to be on the front line to be useful. Dispatchers are needed, as are people in the background of a scene to organize and co-ordinate services.

Yes, there are women firefighters. If you want to join, call the local department and ask how to apply. They provide training. This is not quick or easy training, but a long-term commitment.

Chapter 21

Part of a Neighborhood

In part, your neighborhood is what you make of it, what you contribute to it. If it is a safe place already, thank your neighbors and your local law enforcement. If it isn't, do something about it.

Safe Houses for children

Nothing is worse for a small child than to come home from school or play to find no one at home. It is terrifying. Have a contingency plan that the child understands and can use. Make arrangements with a trusted (by you and the child) neighbor in case this should happen. If you are called out on a sudden emergency for one child and can't get a hold of the other to explain, at least the child knows he or she has a safe place to go to wait for Mom or Dad. And you, the parent, know where to find your child. Do trust a child's instincts regarding other people. Respect their feelings as these can be surprisingly accurate, seeing something in a person that you can't.

> Years ago, when I was a teen, I found a six-year-old child crying alone on the sidewalk. His mother wasn't home yet and he was beyond bewildered and frightened. He didn't know where to go nor what to do. Don't let that happen to your child.

Many neighborhoods have established their own system of safe houses, with decals in the windows or doors identifying them, for children who feel they are being stalked or harassed on their way home from school or other locations. If one isn't established in your neighborhood, consider starting such a system.

> My own son refused to join the local boy scouts and wouldn't tell me why, until it came out that one of the boy scout leaders was a pedophile. He knew something was wrong from stories the other boys told and didn't want to be a part of it. Fortunately, I didn't push the issue at the time.

Heads Up
If you notice something amiss with a neighbor's house, don't hesitate to call the police or appropriate emergency responders. You may help protect a neighbor some day, just as they may protect you.

Don't be afraid to seek these homes out and introduce yourself and your children. Kids need to know they are not abandoned and alone if a strange car approaches and asks them "for directions" or spooks the child. I can remember from my own childhood, a five-year-old sister of a classmate who was almost abducted from her front yard, but had enough savvy to scream bloody murder and run for her front door, frightening the man away.

Neighborhood Watches

Neighborhood watches not only look out for children but property and anything else unusual happening in their neighborhood. If there is one in your neighborhood, don't hesitate to become a part of it. Check with your local police department to find out who is running the program. If there isn't one, perhaps you should start one.

Curb appeal and fitting in

If you move into a neighborhood with manicured lawns, lovely gardens and expect to put up a gaudy lawn display, you may be in for a tough time from your neighbors. Not only are you interfering with their already established "look" but you are also lessening the value of their property.

Presumably, you moved into the neighborhood because you liked it the way it was. By fitting in, you increase everyone's property values including your own.

If you wish to do something drastic, you might check with the neighbors first and get a feel for their reactions. It wouldn't do to build the biggest and meanest tree fort in history in the middle of your front yard, in a neighborhood where views are a critical part of the beauty. You might have a revolt on your hands. It could also be construed as a danger.

In the reverse, if you move to a neighborhood that isn't up to par, but has promise and you lead the way to cleaning it up, you may find your neighbors pitching in and doing their share too. Sometimes, it only needs a leader to get the action moving constructively.

Yard maintenance

Definitely a part of fitting in with your neighborhood. You will be expected to maintain your yard as your neighbors do. The grass will have to be mowed on a regular schedule, the weeds trimmed.

Unless you live in the country where no one can see your house from the road, you are rather stuck with this routine. If you can't manage the lawn, hire a local kid to mow and trim for you. If you prefer to hire pros, do it. My brother made money as a kid by mowing neighbor's lawns.

Heads Up
Your best weapon is knowledge. Educate yourself.

Of course, it is one way to meet your neighbors to spend time on your lawn and chat with the people passing by. You become available for conversation and will get to know your neighbors that much faster.

What is yours, what is mine

Respecting your neighbor's property and property rights is paramount to living in a neighborhood. You sure don't want somebody slapping signs on your property without permission, or dashing about in your back yard without asking you. Same goes for your neighbors.

Fences—keep them on your side

Would you like to put up a fence? Will it be in keeping with the neighborhood? If you live in a wide open backyard type of neighborhood, you may incur some nasty feelings if you put up a huge privacy fence when a small picket fence may be more appropriate.

Make sure that any fence you propose to put up is on your property, not encroaching on your neighbor's property. If the fence does happen to get on their side, they have every right to remove it.

Property lines—where are they?

When you bought your home and property, the deed will tell you exactly where your property lines are. But reading degrees and lines is different than actually walking the lines and knowing where the little marker stakes are. You should know where the boundaries are. Ask your neighbor to show you what or where his/her boundaries are. Presumably they are yours too. Unless, of course, someone got it wrong. When it comes to legal stuff—get a surveyor on the job.

Zoning ordinances—how they affect you

Zoning

In the larger sense, zoning protects you and your community from senseless, reckless development. Isn't that why you moved there in the first place?

All land is divided into zones for specific uses: residential, business, agriculture, manufacturing, mixtures of residential and agriculture and so on. The zoning ordinances are designed for a community's planned and orderly growth.

Ordinances keep houses in Residential areas and massive stores in Business districts. It wouldn't do to have a massive "box store" planted in the middle of a residential neighborhood. The traffic would be horrendous, not to mention what it would do to your property values.

In scenic areas, zoning helps keep the open fields open, the mountaintops empty of ill-placed houses, the farms farming. All around the country, communities are using zoning to protect habitat, historic places, wetlands, scenic areas, and other treasures from random development.

If you move to a special place, you don't expect it to be developed into something entirely different. You don't move to the country to discover a developer has just decided to create another city and despoil the area.

Easements and rights-of-way

It is quite possible that there are public pathways around your neighborhood. The land is owned by someone, maybe even you. In Vermont, we are currently struggling with the "ancient roads" issue. These are historic roads that were once used, but have faded into history. For example, we own a tiny piece of the Old Boston Post Road which runs the entire length of the state—if you could find it on a map. Trouble is, can you find it on a map somewhere? Maybe not, but that doesn't mean it still isn't a "public road" that can be used by the public without your consent. If you happen to have built a house on the road, you may find yourself with a title insurance issue.

This is especially true in the country. You may buy a nice piece of property only to find that your cute little driveway that goes up to your side door is actually and legally, someone else's driveway to the property behind you. They just haven't built their house yet. That is a right-of-way written into your property deed. And that little driveway could be a 50-foot wide right-of-way! There isn't much you can do about it either.

It does help to be aware of those "little" provisions. Your best defense is to educate yourself on exactly what your property is, where it is in relation to property lines, and find out about these potential surprises.

Easements are the right of the town to do something on your property—but only to a point. For example, you live on a small road in a quiet community. But the traffic is increasing noticeably. The town fathers decide that the road needs to be widened. And they may have the right-of-way to do it. The act of widening the road may take up half of your front yard, but too bad for you.

Disagree?
If you live in a small town and disagree with the town on any road width issues, a good place for info is to check the historic road surveys in the town clerk's office.

As a child I remember our little road became a thoroughfare for commuters. Our neighborhood was visited by the endless sounds of trees being felled, cement trucks and bulldozers and other large equipment as our rough, but paved road became a wide, slick commuter road.

Pets are neighbors too

So you have pets. Cool. We have lots of pets. Your pets are neighbors too. And how they fit into the neighbor is quite important. It doesn't do to get a vicious dog "as protection" in a neighborhood where kids are playing everywhere. What if the dog gets loose and hurts someone?

Golden Leash

You don't want to be annoyed by someone else's dog anymore than they wish to be annoyed by yours.

Leash laws

Most communities have leash laws to protect non-owners from other people's pets. If you don't abide by them, your pet can be taken from you. Or you may have to pay a fine. Find this out ahead of time from the town offices.

Essentially, the law will read that your pet dog must remain on a leash while outside—at all times. Or some variation on this—generally meaning that your pet must be under your control. Perhaps the law has variations on the time of year. In parts of rural Vermont, it depends on where and the season. During the winter and early spring, the leash laws are in effect to prevent dogs from ganging up and chasing deer to their deaths by exhaustion in deep snow. Sounds reasonable.

Poop Laws

Face it, do you like stepping in dog poop? Nah. To make sure no one has to deal with that situation, pooper-scooper laws have become more prevalent. Again, check at the town offices for your locale. This applies mostly in urban and suburban communities where walking the dog is the only way to get the dog out for a potty break.

Barking

No one likes a dog that barks its brains out endlessly. If your dog does this, you won't make a lot of friends with your neighbors. The smart thing to do would be to find the root of the barking and deal with it. Dogs have feelings too. A lonely dog barks. Get the dog a companion. Or perhaps, find another loving home for the dog.

Part VI

Growing Your Home

Chapter 22

Planning Is Everything

Unless you are some sort of building genius and do it yourself and have plenty of resources in case you foul up, you do need to plan for every bit of your project.

Ordinances, zoning and licenses

You or your contractor needs to check with the town offices to see if your project is allowed. There are "setback" rules and regulations, road-cuts to consider if you are adding another road to the site, and a variety of other possible restrictions. Perhaps there are height restrictions to consider.

Does this project fit in with the current zoning laws? If you are adding an office addition, are home offices allowed? Are you adding a home business that generates traffic to your home? That could be restricted.

All these points must be checked before you get started on your project. You don't want any surprises after you've laid out a wad of money on planning.

Discuss it, plan it, measure for it

The first thing to decide is what exactly you want done. Make another one of those endless lists of what you really want, what you would love to have and what you can't do without. Speak with everyone involved with the project. If there are family members, let everyone have their say.

DIY?
Even if you plan to do this yourself, you still have to go through the process: planning, budgets, permits, then doing it.

Planning is Everything

Decide what you can do without if the bids come in too high.

Spend time planning for this project. Cut out pictures of what exactly you want, if you have to. Make a collection of photos to refer to.

Let the designer, architect, builder, or whoever is doing the design know *exactly* what it is you want.

It will cost you plenty to have a contractor build what he or she *thinks* you want, but if it isn't what you want, it's because you didn't spell out your desires exactly before the project began.

While you can do a bang-up job of measuring, make sure the pros do their measuring before any work is done. You may not realize there are other things they have to measure for, or make adjustments for.

Talk to your Realtor® first

This may sound stupid, until you realize that if you build an extraordinary addition making your little home a palace, and you live in an area where most of the houses are little homes, you will not get back your investment in the addition. Find out if your proposed project fits the location, if you will get your investment back at sale time, or anything else the agent or broker might have to offer in the way of information.

Say you live in a community of $100k homes and you build a $100k addition to your house. It is now worth $200k—maybe. It is unlikely that a buyer will pay that much for an expensive house in an inexpensive neighborhood.

Working out projected costs

The rule of thumb when planning additions or remodeling projects is to add at least 20% onto the top of any contract or pricing as a contingency. Without fail, you will use it. Whatever price the contractor comes up with, add that 20% to it. Think of it as a safety cushion. If you don't use it for the project—think vacation!

Want to save money? Consider making your home more energy efficient in the process. There may be grants or special loans available to upgrade your home. Perhaps even tax credits or considerations.

Be reasonable and flexible

You may not wish to tear apart your house in the dead of winter, if you live up north. Some jobs work out quite well in the winter. Contractors love to have "winter work"—that which can be done inside where it is warm and their crews can work without threat of snow, rain, wind and other nasty attacks by nature. If your project is a great winter job, bear with the contractor if this is suggested.

Consider structural integrity

It doesn't make sense to put a huge second floor onto a small home with a foundation and walls that can't hold the weight of the proposed project. Just as you wouldn't put a one-ton slate roof on a tiny house with paper thin walls, you need to be aware of structural elements in the house that can't be changed.

For instance, there are "load-bearing" walls, and "non-load-bearing" walls within a structure. Guess which ones you can't play with? You got it. The load-bearing walls are carrying the roof or floors above them. Without their support, you've lost the skeleton of your house. If you insist on changing load-bearing walls, you will have to make some serious adjustments and considerations in your plans—and be prepared to pay for them.

Materials

Where you buy your materials can mean a huge difference in cost. Contractors can and do buy locally, using contractor discounts. Their purchase volume is so high that even small local businesses can afford to offer the discount. If you have chosen your contractor well, then trust your contractor to get the best price possible.

If you are planning a big project you are doing alone, speak first with your local supply houses and ask about discounts for a project of your size. If you are using a contractor, this part is taken care of.

And, yes Contractors are allowed to make a reasonable profit and to pay their employees well. A happy work crew is "cheaper" in the long run than a miserable crew making a mess of your planned job.

Don't be foolish and demand "cheaper" goods to lower the price. There is a difference between "cheaper" and top-quality-but-not-as-fancy items. For example, you want solid gold faucets in your new bathroom. (Don't we all wish we could afford them!) But your budget says brass. Will you fight for the solid gold fixtures but stint on something more important like using sub-quality pipes that don't show—and pay the endless repair costs later? Not a wise choice.

Stages

You could always plan your job in reasonable stages as your budget and/or dreams allow.

Here's an example from real life: There are too many times when Peter has been asked to cut back on quality masonry, as in "make it cheaper!" to find that the homeowner is spending $3,000 on a small countertop of granite. Or as much as the chimney for bathroom fixtures of gold (seriously). The problem with this scenario is simple: a lousy masonry job can kill you. Scaling down to brass instead of gold fixtures won't. Fortunately, Peter doesn't skimp on quality—ever.

If you want your project to be grand, but your budget won't allow it, scale the whole project back, leave some of the extras out, or wait until you can afford it as you want it. Invariably, there are extras that can be added later without compromising the project. Don't ever skimp on the basics and structure of the job.

Get your permits

When you are ready to jump in—by all means, get that permit. You can't start without it. Head down to the town or city clerk's office and apply for your permit.

If your GC does that... let him or her at it!

Chapter 23

Finding a Contractor

First of all, contractors are human beings with families to support, too. If their prices seem high, consider that they do have overhead and have to pay their employees well to attract the best. Blue collar professions may not be as glamorous as white collar jobs, but they are entitled to good wages and benefits. Just think, if everyone had "glamorous" jobs, there wouldn't be anyone to fix our cars, fix our houses, or clean up our garbage. These jobs and workers deserve respect, too.

Even plumbers and electricians require training that costs money. More importantly, if a non-trained "plumber" or "electrician" does the job and botches it, fixing the error will cost you far more than doing it right the first time. Same for any contracted job.

Choose your contractor wisely

Don't even consider choosing one who comes to your door and tells you that you *need* a job done. That is a huge red-flag warning. These guys usually skip town after they collect a big upfront payment.

Don't just pick out the biggest ad in the yellow pages. Sometimes the biggest ad is bought by the most desperate. The truly excellent contractors don't always need to advertise too heavily, they are booked solid all season.

Ask your friends, neighbors, co-workers or anyone else you know who has had work done, about contractors.

Big job, little job

Little Jobs

If your job only involves one sub-contractor to do the job, call the sub directly.

A major renovation or addition requires the skills and talents of a general or remodeling contractor. Adding a chimney/fireplace, fixing plumbing, electric repairs, or other smaller jobs don't need a general contractor. Go directly to the subcontractor.

General contractors add their overhead (around 10% to a job or sub's bid), which you pay. On a big job, they are vital and worth their weight in platinum. If a job requires more than one sub with coordination between many subs, look for a general contractor. You won't regret it.

Finding a contractor

Scams

Beware of Fix It Scams, they are still frequent. If you have any doubts about who is offering to do a job for you, tell the "sub" that you will call their office. Get their number, (license plate as well as phone number) then call the BBB or even the police.

Do not EVER let them inside your house—period!

Do not, under any circumstance, say "Sure, just fix it," to someone who shows up at your front door telling you your roof needs fixing, or some other bogus repair. If someone tries that on you, tell them you will call their references, or call the BBB about them, or tell them you will investigate their company before you allow them to touch your abode. If that doesn't scare them off, call the police.

Check with the Better Business Bureau

Visit in-progress or finished jobs and get references from potential contractors. Look carefully at what was done. Don't do a quick once-over and think it looks great. Look closely at what was done. Seams match? Did they cut corners? If you know someone in the building business, ask them for advice or take them along. Ask the people for whom the work is being done about their job. Is the contractor easy to have around? Cooperative?

Check with the local National Association of Home Builders (NAHB) or other local home builders association in your area. The NAHB's website is listed in Resources. It is loaded with information for consumers.

Check with lumber and supply stores

That's where the contractors buy their material. Most suppliers have their customers' business cards tacked on a board somewhere.

How can you compare?

Check out a variety of stores and compare prices. The closer you get to the source of the material, the less expensive it is. Stores selling only small quantities of goods usually buy their stuff from a middle-level supplier, who in turn has marked up what was purchased from the original source. If your potential contractor buys from the original source, you'll pay less for the material and still get excellent quality supplies, at a fair price. It's a win/win situation.

To make the situation a bit muddled, many local contractors buy from the same hardware stores you do, but these hardware stores give them a "contractor's discount" which can be quite substantial, making their bids comparable to a contractor buying elsewhere—usually. It's worth asking.

However, one contractor confronts "the mega-store factor" all the time. "My customers tell me 'I can buy for less at the DIY mega store.' What the customer doesn't figure in are the ancillary expenses. Examples are windows or doors. A customer just told me she could get a window there for $139 and why was I charging $288. Differences were my window included Low E film, argon gas, grilles and screens, casing around the window, a window sill, apron board *and* installation. Items the mega store doesn't include on doors are the outside light with the door light switch as well as the electrical outlet outside door, trim, header, painting." If you are capable of installing the door, as well as all the other parts that go with it, fine. If not, or you can't be bothered, hire the best contractor.

Fair bids

Supplies for a job are usually marked up 10% to the customer. That overhead pays for the office structure, insurance, running equipment, trucks, telephone and other business expenses. That's only fair, as every other business incorporates the same expenses in their prices as well.

You and the Contractor

If the contractor treats you as if you are a dummy or gives you the "little lady" treatment, *find another contractor*. You don't have to deal with that attitude. Excellent contractors treat everyone as intelligent but perhaps uninformed about what is going on. It would help if you did some homework on the subject beforehand. Try the internet or library or check out bookstores. There are plenty of books on most subjects about building or house maintenance.

Don't be taken in by a contractor with the gift of gab, when he tries to sell you a lousy job, or a low bid that backfires. We know contractors who are quite adept at conning people into a job, only the people find out later they've been had. Some of the most reticent contractors are the best. Some of the gabbiest are the worst. It's your final decision. Does the contractor do some of the work himself? Or are you getting gabbed at by a front man? We know several contractors who have "retired" from actual construction work themselves but have others do the work for them and quite literally "support" them. They do the slick gab, based on their previous work history, but what they promise isn't necessarily what you will see happen.

Meet the Subs
Sub-contractors are human, too. They appreciate being consulted directly rather than being ignored when it comes to finding out exactly what work you want done.

Follow the Building and Safety Codes

Your safety can be at stake when choosing a contractor. A badly built chimney can burn down your house. Incorrectly installed plumbing can flood your house. Improperly installed wiring can burn your house down.

These codes exist for a reason. If you have questions, check with your state's offices dealing with contractors and building inspections.

Insurance

Does your contractor carry all the necessary insurance? Ask them up front. You can get a copy of their coverage from their insurance company. It is to protect you and your property as well as the contractor's. If a workman breaks a leg on your property—who is paying for this? If someone breaks a window dropping a tool, who pays? Make sure they have coverage!

> My husband, a contractor, has been outbid on jobs in the past. In one instance, we have found out, after the fact, that the lower bidder didn't carry insurance—the exact difference between our bid and the other.

Getting bids: cheaper isn't always better

If you don't like a price, ask other contractors to bid on your project. Let the contractor know up front if others are bidding on it. Get written estimates or proposals for comparison. Ask if your job is too big, or too small for them. Smaller contractors can have a more personalized relationship with a client, especially if the job is small. You will get listened to. A huge company may need to keep dozens of workers busy and a small "insignificant" job could get lost in the shuffle. This isn't always true, but it is up to you to judge from conversations with the contractors. Further investigate the ones you feel comfortable with.

Judging bids

When the bids come in, throw out the highest and lowest and pick the best from the ones in the middle. If a contractor is really lower than the rest, something is missing. For example, maybe the contractor has "forgotten" something important (I know a contractor who does this religiously) and while his initial contract price was very low, you end up being "change ordered" into paying far more than you would have if you had accepted the bid of a contractor in the middle, or even the most expensive.

Make sure that all bidders are bidding on exactly the same project! Is one bid less than another because the material is of lesser quality? If so, you may be paying more for shoddy goods in the end.

Bids

Is everyone bidding on the same project?

Do they carry insurance?

Are they bidding on the same material?

Can you see some of their finished jobs?

Years ago, my husband, a masonry contractor, was asked to bid on building a single-flue chimney for a woodstove. The sons of the elderly woman needing the chimney decided they didn't want to squander money on Mom's chimney and chose another contractor who was several hundred dollars less. At the end of the heating season, Peter received a call, could he come and fix the chimney? It didn't work and was already falling apart. So—how much did they save? Really?

Deadlines

In building and remodeling, deadlines are something to aim for, NOT an absolute. Plan your own life around that fact.

Perhaps double the amount of time you planned for the job, then you'll be happily surprised when it comes in "on time"— close to the original time.

Planning and Dates

As much as you will hate hearing this: *don't ask a contractor to hold to an absolute date for the job.* They can give you an approximate date. The contractors will try their darndest to comply and accommodate you and your schedule. Just be forewarned that weather, job delays and other factors can seriously ruin schedules. If it is raining and you are having an outside job done, don't expect your contractor to pour concrete or mix cement in a rainstorm. It is an exercise in futility. Every rainstorm backs up roofing contractors. Believe me, you don't want your roof exposed and leaking during a downpour. Dumb.

Contracts

Get one and stick with it—especially on big jobs. Have it checked by a lawyer you trust, who is experienced in these types of contracts. Make sure you don't pay most of the contract price up front. That, too, is a red flag. Roughly 20% of a job is normal up-front money. You don't want the contractor to pay off someone else's bill with your deposit, then not have your money to buy your supplies.

On the Job

Be kind and thoughtful. Don't assume the contractor is ripping you off. If you have chosen your contractor wisely, don't second guess him or her. Micro-managing a job can lead to extra expenses no one had planned on. If you have children, keep them out of the way.

Oops!

On the other hand, if you see things that aren't right, say something immediately! Don't wait until it's too late to correct the situation. Document things that don't look or seem right to you.

Take a walk through the site daily to see how the job is progressing. Don't be afraid to talk to the workers. I can't tell you how often owners will speak to the boss or foreman instead of to the subcontractor directly doing the job, in front of the sub—but ignoring him as if he or she were worthless. Bad idea. If you have questions, ask now.

Help keep the workflow flowing

There's more to "building it" than just hiring a contractor. There are things you, the homeowner, have to do to help keep the workflow steady and the atmosphere comfortable to work in.

You need to have the workspace ready for the contractor when the crew arrives. That means, get out of the way and allow the crew a safe place to work—a place where "the public" isn't milling around and getting in the way.

Do offer coffee and snacks. Make your work site a pleasant place to come to. What you offer as refreshment goes a very long way to making your job a place to look forward to work in. As a result, the crew will do beyond their best to show their appreciation.

Cleaning up

Usually, the crew leaves the work site "broom clean" at the end of the day. That doesn't mean spotless. That isn't

Warning
Don't interrupt the workers or distract them unless absolutely necessary.

their job. It also doesn't mean you can allow anyone to wander through the site and touch or play with the crew's tools. It's a safety thing.

By all means, go look at the work being done. If you don't understand something, ask at the next opportunity. Understand that you are paying them for their *time* on the job. Be brief.

If there are any requests from you, make sure you make them ahead of time. i.e., supposing you need to work on your computer, but the electrician is coming and must shut down the entire household electric—make sure you can work this out with the general contractor and sub ahead of time, so there aren't any surprises.

Offerings

A pot of coffee available for the workers is always welcome, especially first thing in the morning. They won't abuse the offer and you may find your job going better than you expected.

Subcontractors

If you are working with a general contractor (or GC), the GC will handle the scheduling of the subs. If the job is small enough that the use of a GC isn't warranted, then call the sub yourself.

Understand that subs have crews, too. Maybe only one or two people. They have to keep their people working and earning a living. If you can't make up your mind, for one reason or another, you delay everyone. That backs up all the work to be done after that sub. Not to mention jobs following yours.

Know exactly what you want when you make your final decision, but also know the implications of those decisions. If you choose a rare tile to be installed, and it takes six weeks to arrive on special order, but the tile contractor needs it in two weeks, you have a problem. Will another tile do as well? You may need to be flexible as well. If you insist on those rare tiles, then you will have to wait until all the crews can be lined up again, because it's guaranteed they will all start working on another job.

Payments

Pay on time as per your contract. It's quite fair to pay something up front if the contractor needs it—not all of the money, mind you—only some—as agreed. If the job is a long one, it is reasonable to pay something, as agreed, weekly or bi-weekly. Don't forget, the contractor still has to pay the subs and his own employees on time. The final costs to borrow money to pay them while your job is continuing comes from your checkbook one way or another.

It isn't unheard of that if the homeowner doesn't pay on time, the contractor walks away to do a job that will pay.

Don't expect the contractor to do anything for free. You can't just add a "Gee, while you're at it..." and expect them to be happy about it—or to do it. It still costs the contractor money and time. His time and money are just as valuable as yours.

Don't hesitate
If you have a problem, speak up immediately. Your contractor should be your friend, not your enemy.

Do-It List

√ *do your contractor research*

√ *get a copy of their coverage* from their insurance company

√ *check with the Better Business Bureau or local NAHB*

√ *have your financing ready* and be prepared to pay on time as agreed

√ *sign the contract* after you have thoroughly read it and agree, and hopefully have a lawyer check it

√ *be flexible* as to schedule

√ *keep an eye on the job*

√ *speak up if necessary*—stay informed

√ *Pay on time!*

Maurie Harrington, Artist

Maurie Harrington, The Traveling Artist, has been painting as long as she can remember. While her studio is in Killington, Vermont, she paints globally, having painted her way through Croatia, Belgium, Egypt, France, Africa, Greece, Crete, Indonesia and Newfoundland to name a few.

The cover painting is of a cottage on the grounds of the Fisk Farm located on Vermont's Isle la Motte where Maurie gives painting lessons every summer.

Maurie's deep-seated love of nature captures that beauty with her special artist's touch. From mountain vistas and quiet forests, to vibrant flowers, she captures and conveys the essence of place and time.

Although she exhibits her work throughout New England, her work graces homes internationally. She is well known for her watercolor workshops held at her studio and in North Hero, Vermont. She has illustrated several books, including contributing drawings in four editions (1998–2001) of Conde Nast's *Best of Gourmet*.

She frequently lectures to interested groups, offering her art, photographs and videos of her trips.

She holds a Masters Degree in Art from the University of Norwich, Vermont and a Bachelor of Fine Arts from the University of Hartford, Connecticut.

She can be reached at:

Maurie Harrington
PO Box 176
Killington, Vermont 05751-0176
Telephone: 802-422-7756

maurie@maurieharrington.com

www.maurieharrington.com

Kitty Werner, Author

I was first drawn to construction when my father decided our side porch would make a dandy office for himself. Then seven years old, I offered my services by hanging around until he found something useful for me to do.

About this time, I had received a beautiful little doll for Christmas. Having a younger brother, and a sister with a doll, we used our dolls to play kickball. After a few too many innings, poor Ginsia's leg flew up in the air with the ball. I took her apart and wired her back together. When the arms came off, I used a rubberband—as the manufacturer had. She was the perfect doll.

I was hired by a flooring company to sell flooring, but ended up running the warehouse. I furnished my first townhouse with scraps of carpet, padding, carpet samples and plywood. Sold all of it when I moved to Germany when I married Peter, a German mason (now a masonry contractor in Vermont).

Back in the States, Peter and I ran an old Vermont farmhouse as a ski lodge for a winter. We ran out of water the first day we had guests (Christmas Day)! Dealing with the fix-it issues of old dryers, temperamental heating systems, cranky plumbing, mazes of "put-together" pipes and wires, wells, and chimneys was an education in survival!

Eventually we bought our own house. As the family grew, the house grew. We fixed and added electric wiring, replumbed fixtures, finished off a bathroom, added a large addition, dealt with lightning storms blasting our water supply, downed electric lines, and all manner of exciting events. This advice comes from experience. We've lived it.

As to the writing parts: I've been writing features and books since 1990. When I thought I had a "great novel" to sell, I started The Dorothy Canfield Fisher Writers Conference that ran for eight years (1990–1997), and where I got my first paid writing job: editing the bi-yearly *The Official Directory to U.S. Flea Markets* published by Crown, formerly Random House for six editions. Since then I've been a newspaper editor, a columnist, and now, I design and publish books for other small presses as well.

Mercifully, that novel is still hidden away.

Resources

Chapter 2 — Get Functional
American Association of Poison Control Centers.............. 800-222-1222
....www.aapcc.org
American Board of Medical Specialties 866-ASK-ABMS
....www.abms.org
AMA Physcian Select..www.ama-assn.org

Chapter 4 — Safety and Sanity
Kidde ....www.kiddeus.com
U.S. Fire Administration....................... www.usfa.dhs.gov/kids/flash.shtm
Jomy Safety Products — fire escape ladders.......................www.jomy.com
Radon Info (EPA) .... www.epa.gov/iaq/radon
National Safety Council (Radon info) 800-SOS-RADON
....www.nsc.org
Radon Kits ....www.nsc.org/ehc/radon/coupon.htm

Chapter 5 — Beat Catastrophe—Insure it!
Consumer's Reports.................................... www.consumerreports.org
The Insurance Network.. www.insure.com
FEMA — Nat'l Flood Insurance Program....... 1-888-CALLFLOODx445
Flood Smart .... www.floodsmart.gov
CLUE — your house insurance rating.................... www.choicetrust.com
US Geological Survey—Earthquakes .... http://earthquake.usgs.gov/

Chapter 6 — The Water Works
Gordon Tool Co – shut-off valve wrench............................949-552-7613
....www.gordonwrench.com

Chapter 7 — Staying Warm, Staying Cool
U.S. Dept of Energy .... www.eere.energy.gov/
Home Energy Magazine.. http://homeenergy.org
American Council for an Energy-Efficient Economy .... www.aceee.org

Chapter 9 — Preparing for Repairs
Energy Star Ratings .... www.energystar.gov
Leatherman Tools ....www.leatherman.com

Chapter 11 — Yearly Check-Up
National Association of Home Builders............................www.nahb.org
Koolseal – roofing information .... www.koolseal.com

Chapter 12 — Energy Efficiency
Efficiency Vermont .... www.efficiencyvermont.com
Energy Star Ratings .... www.energystar.gov

Chapter 13 — Go Green, Go Healthy
Seventh Generation.................................... www.seventhgeneration.com

ᴊapter 14 — Pesky Things

University of NC Bug Info .... www.ces.ncsu.edu/depts/ent/notes/

National Pest Control .... www.pestworld.org

Chapter 15 — Get Out Alive

Jomy Safety Products (ladders) .... www.jomy.com

Chapter 16 — First Aid and Emergency Kits

Red Cross .... www.redcross.org

The Sportsman's Guide .... www.sportsmansguide.com

FEMA .... www.fema.gov

Chapter 17 — Suddenly On Your Own

NOAA .... www.noaa.gov

Homeland Security's Ready site .... www.Ready.gov

Chapter 19 — Schools

Center for Education Reform .... www.edreform.com

Education Week and Teacher Magazine .... www.edweek.org

Independent Schools Associations of the Central States ..... www.isacs.org
.... (630) 971-3581

New England Association of Schools and Colleges .... www.neasc.org
.... (781) 271-0022

About.com .... http://privateschool.about.com
.... http://homeschooling.about.com

Home Education Magazine .... www.homeedmag.com

Chapter 23 — Finding a Contractor

National Association of Home Builders .... www.nahb.org

A Note: As of the printing of this book, November 2006, the above references are correct. We cannot be responsible for any changes since then.

Books

About the House with Henri de Marne, Upper Access Publishing, $19.95, ISBN 978-0-942679-30-4

The Home Energy Diet, Paul Scheckel, New Society Publishers, $18.95, ISBN 978-0-86472-530-1

The following books have superb information on environmental toxins and their affect on our health:

It's My Ovaries, Stupid! Elizabeth Lee Vliet, M.D., HER Place Press, $19.95, ISBN 978-1-933213-3-3

The Savvy Woman's Guide to PCOS, Elizabeth Lee Vliet, M.D., HER Place Press, $18.95, ISBN 1-933213-01-9

Utility Company Phone List

Telephone
Company Name_____
Account Number _____
Phone Number _____
Contact _____

Electric
Company Name_____
Account Number _____
Phone Number _____
Contact _____

Fuel
Company Name_____
Account Number _____
Phone Number _____
Contact _____

Plumber
Company Name_____
Account Number _____
Phone Number _____
Contact _____

Electrician
Company Name_____
Account Number _____
Phone Number _____
Contact _____

A/C
Company Name_____
Account Number _____
Phone Number _____
Contact _____

_____
Company Name_____
Account Number _____
Phone Number _____
Contact _____